# HOW PICTURES COMPLETE US

# HOW PICTURES COMPLETE US

## The Beautiful, the Sublime, and the Divine

PAUL CROWTHER

STANFORD UNIVERSITY PRESS
STANFORD, CALIFORNIA

Stanford University Press
Stanford, California

Printed in the United States of America on acid-free, archival-quality paper

Library of Congress Cataloging-in-Publication Data

Crowther, Paul, author.
How pictures complete us : the beautiful, the sublime, and the divine / Paul Crowther.
pages cm
Includes bibliographical references and index.
ISBN 978-0-8047-9573-9 (cloth : alk. paper)—
ISBN 978-0-8047-9846-4 (pbk. : alk. paper)—
ISBN 978-0-8047-9858-7 (electronic)
1. Art, Modern—Philosophy. 2. Pictures—Philosophy. 3. Aesthetics, Modern. 4. Art
and religion. I. Title.
N6350.C76 2016
700.9'04—dc23
2015030664

Typeset by Bruce Lundquist in 10/14 Minion Pro

I mean by a picture a beautiful, romantic dream of something that never was, never will be—in a light better than any light that ever shone—in a land no one can define or remember, only desire— and the forms divinely beautiful.

—Edward Coley Burne-Jones

# CONTENTS

Illustrations     ix

Acknowledgments     xi

Introduction: Pictorial Beauty and Aesthetic Transcendence     1

1    Ideal Beauty and Classic Art: A Philosophical Vindication     11

2    Pictorial Art and Metaphysical Beauty     37

3    Transcendent Subjectivity: Kant and the Pictorial Sublime     57

4    Color-Field Abstraction and the Mystical Sublime     79

5    Holistic Beauty at the Limits of Art:
Photocollage, Painting, and Digital Imagery     107

6    Perspective and Icon: Jean-Luc Marion's Theology of Painting     125

7    Metaphysics and Theology of Pictorial Art     143

Notes     161

Index     173

# ILLUSTRATIONS

Figure 1.   Piero della Francesca, *Baptism of Christ* (1448–1450)                27

Figure 2.   Nicolas Poussin, *A Bacchanalian Revel Before a Term* (1632)          29

Figure 3.   Frederic, Lord Leighton, *Captive Andromache* (1888)                  30

Figure 4.   Ian Hamilton Finlay, *Five Finials* (2001)                            35

Figure 5.   Edward Coley Burne-Jones, *Study for Love Amongst
            the Ruins* (1867–1870)                                                44

Figure 6.   Roger Fry, *View of Royat from the Parc Montjuizot* (1934)            47

Figure 7.   James Tissot, *What Our Lord Saw from the Cross
            (Ce que voyait Notre-Seigneur sur la Croix)* (c. 1886–1894)           68

Figure 8.   John Martin, *The Evening of the Deluge* (1834)                       72

Figure 9.   Alfred William Hunt, *A Stream in a Moorland Landscape*
            (c. 1870)                                                            72

Figure 10.  Bracha Lichtenberg Ettinger, *Autistwork n. 1* (1992–1993)           75

Figure 11.  Bracha Lichtenberg Ettinger, *Eurydice n. 23* (1994–1998)            75

Figure 12.  Barnet Newman, *Stations of the Cross: First Station* (1958)          89

Figure 13.  Barnet Newman, *Stations of the Cross: Third Station*
            (1958–1966)                                                          90

Figure 14.  Barnet Newman, *Stations of the Cross: Ninth Station*
            (1958–1966)                                                          91

Figure 15.  Barnet Newman, *Stations of the Cross: Tenth Station*
            (1958–1966)                                                          92

Figure 16.  Mark Rothko, *Light Red over Black* (1957)                           98

Figure 17.  Mark Rothko, *Black on Maroon* (1958)                               101

Figure 18.  Mark Rothko, *Red on Maroon* (1959)                                 101

Figure 19.  Arlo P. Darkly, *The Terminator* (c. 1993)                          112

# ACKNOWLEDGMENTS

Chapter 5 was first published as "Art and the Reconfiguration of Contemporary Experience," in *Aesthetics as Philosophy*, ed. A. Erjavec (Ljubljana: SAZU, 1999), pp. 127–135. It has been extensively revised and extended for inclusion in the present volume.

# HOW PICTURES COMPLETE US

# INTRODUCTION

*Pictorial Beauty and Aesthetic Transcendence*

Pictures exist to be looked at. But our wanting to look at them is provoked by *how* they make things visible, as well as by the stories they tell. This making-visible is of major philosophical interest. It is hardly surprising, then, that in recent years the concept of pictorial representation has been one of the most fruitfully explored areas of philosophical aesthetics.

Nelson Goodman's *Languages of Art* (1968) was important in stimulating widespread interest in the epistemology and semantics of picturing.[1] This interest has continued, resulting in many important monographs—notably by Kendall Walton, Robert Hopkins, Dominic McIver Lopes, and Patrick Maynard.[2] The continental tradition has also considered the philosophical significance of pictorial images, but in contexts mainly concerning their ontology or broader cultural significance. Works by Maurice Merleau-Ponty and, more recently, Gilles Deleuze, Jean-Luc Nancy, and Jacques Rancière have been especially influential.[3] And of course, within the field of art history, pictorial representation is often addressed in terms that consider the philosophical implications of its history. Gombrich's *Art and Illusion* (1960) was an important, pioneering book in this respect, and more recently James Elkins has produced a substantial corpus of important work.[4]

However, there is one aspect of pictorial representation that has received rather less attention, namely, the *distinctive* basis of pictorial art as art. I emphasize "distinctive" here because, while pictorial representation has often been included in general theories of art, there has, in recent times, been much less attention to the aesthetic uniqueness of picture-making. And there is such uniqueness. When a picture represents visible things, it changes how they appear—on the basis of factors distinctive to pictorial media. Among those who have addressed this, Richard Wollheim and Lopes have linked artistic meaning in pictures to the notion of expression.[5] Neither of them, however, has explained what makes expression in pictorial art aesthetically different from that in other art media.[6]

One might, of course, say that the expressiveness of picturing is sufficiently distinguished from that of other things, simply by virtue of arising from pictures rather than from other things. But my point is that the ontological differences at issue here are also responsible for distinctive aesthetic effects. These give pictorial expression a different character from expression arising in other contexts. Indeed, the way such pictorial works move us is often (perhaps even mainly) through a response to the work's overall artistic achievement as such, rather than to specific expressive qualities that might strike us as "happy" or "sad" or "tragic" or whatever. Indeed, when it comes to pictorial artworks of high quality, it is crudely reductive to suppose that their aesthetic significance is explicable using such straightforward expressive terms. Rather, it is the case that, in pictorial art, such expressive qualities are integrated within the distinctive unity of the picture as a whole. ("Distinctive unity" here means both that which is unique to pictorial art as a medium and the artistic style of the particular work.)

I would suggest, then, that it is worth considering an alternative to expression as a basis for explaining the pictorial work's artistic status. The alternative I propose is to focus on the aesthetic grounds of its uniqueness as a medium. This can be done through two moves. The first is a general account of specifically pictorial beauty and how the experience of it can create a sense of psychological completion. The second is more extended (and forms the substance of the present work). It explores how this completion is achieved in distinctive ways, through pictorial beauty's modes of *aesthetic transcendence*. These involve a felt symbolic "going-beyond" our finite limitations, together with (in some circumstances) a felt communion with the divine. Each artistic medium is able to evoke such transcendence on its own terms. To show what is special about pictorial art's modes of doing so, I start with the general theory of pictorial beauty mentioned above.

Over the centuries there have, of course, been many theories of the beautiful. Most of them take it to involve harmonious unities of parts and whole

in sensible phenomena (or in imaginatively intended structures such as literature). But problems arise when it comes to defining the wholes and parts in
question, as well as the criterion of "harmonious unity" between them. The
basic idea becomes difficult as soon as one tries to make it precise.

However, this need not be worrisome. The basic idea is flexible enough to
allow different varieties of beauty to be made more specific ontologically—
on the basis of different whole-part/aspect relations, or to put it another way,
on the basis of the different kinds of objects involved. When the objects are
artworks, these varieties will follow the distinctive ontologies of the relevant
media (such as sculpture, architecture, photography, literature, and music) and
some factors that cut across them. It is when we make beauty specific in such
terms that it becomes more philosophically informative.

And so, to the specific case of pictorial representation. This practice does
not center on copying. It involves, rather, the creation of physical surfaces
marked or inscribed so as to suggest the appearance of some recognizable
kind of three-dimensional item or state of affairs. The suggestion is achieved
through features of shape, mass, and spatial detail (in terms of how the surface
is marked) that—allowing for differences of scale, where relevant—are visually
consistent with how an item or state of affairs of the relevant kind *might* appear.
They allow us to see the three-dimensional structure as if it were *in* the surface
(a fact made much of in Richard Wollheim's work).[7]

Of course, such appearances can be wholly accidental—as when we see such
things "in" clouds—but in the case of the picture, its way of being created offers
cues that allow us to read it as created with the intention of suggesting a three-
dimensional content to us. The criteria of such an intention include evidence of
a process of physical construction, of the construction being sited on a treated
plane surface such as a sheet of paper or a stretched canvas, and/or framing de-
vices whereby the virtual three-dimensionality of the pictorial content is both
drawn attention to and demarcated from the "real" three-dimensional visual
world.

The attention in question here focuses on the open, twofold spatial unity of
the picture (a notion that will be a veritable leitmotif in the present work). This
can be illustrated through a contrast. To comprehend the unity of an event, its
constituent parts must be perceived successively in an exact linear temporal
order. To perceive them in any other order will jumble the parts and make the
event unintelligible as an event. In order to recognize the spatial object as a
unity, however, our perception of its parts is not tied to a strict linear order of

successive apprehension. One can start at the middle and move to the top, or at the bottom right, switching to the left and then moving up—or whatever. The unity of the whole, indeed, is recognized as emergent from cumulative perceptions of its different parts. It has an open unity.

In a picture, there are multiple levels to this unity. As a physical thing, it is a plane surface with lines or marks placed or inscribed upon it. As a presentation of virtual three-dimensional content, it has another level of space that appears to be "in" the surface. When focusing specifically on the picture's narrative or informational function, this latter level is the object of our attention. The physical surface is overlooked in favor of the meaning that is emergent from it.

On other occasions, however, the way in which an artist has represented something is a source of great pleasure in its own right. Such enjoyment can center on the appreciation of harmonies of line, shape, and color for their own sake. But this purely formal experience of beauty can be stimulated by many kinds of visible phenomena and is no help in explaining the distinctive beauty of specifically pictorial art.

The distinctively pictorial aspect is enjoyed when we attend to the work's physical spatiality in relation to its illusionistic space and to the meanings of the narratives and/or figures it represents. And since this relation is directed by the artist's own individual handling of the medium itself, the picture is not just a spatial appearance, but a way of making things appear that, at the same time, expresses the aesthetic interests and values of the creator.

What is decisive, in other words, is a complex unity arising from how the picture's physicality, its style of composition and handling, and its virtual content or narrative make one another visible. Here, in other words, the unity of the work is emergent from three different aspects as well as the parts of those aspects. By means of this emergence, pictorial beauty discloses the world in a distinctive way.

Indeed, its uniqueness reaches further. For such beauty makes us attentive to space-occupancy at the level of space itself. The importance of this is that, in the finite world, space-occupancy is the criterion of existence. If something does not occupy space or is not an effect of space-occupying bodies and/or forces, then we have no grounds for saying that it exists. This is more than a dry fact of ontology. Space-occupying phenomena are not only the basis of our physical existence but the site of all the things we do as well. They have existential importance. Indeed, our interactions with landscapes, places, buildings, rooms, animals, and other human beings create meanings that are the very stuff of life. Space-occupancy is so significant as to permeate every aspect of self-consciousness.

Pictorial beauty plays a unique role here, since it transforms how spatial phenomena appear. The artist's style selectively interprets them and heightens their appearance—bringing out features that might otherwise go unnoticed and unappreciated. His or her way of making-visible offers aesthetic and metaphysical insights into different aspects of space-occupancy and our relation to it. Of course, literature also describes things that happen in the spatial world, and music may allude to them, but only visual art presents and transforms space at the level of space itself, through the open unity of its aesthetic objects. Architecture and sculpture also share their three-dimensional character with the real spatial world, but the specific planar basis of pictorial art adds something.

Insofar, then, as pictorial beauty concerns space-occupancy, it engages with spatial phenomena fundamental to our existence in a way that other art media cannot. It should be emphasized, however, that this is not the basis of a hierarchy. For while pictorial art is privileged in terms of space, the other media also have their own unique ways of being beautiful. They engage with other fundaments of human existence.

Having established the distinctiveness of pictorial beauty, it is clear that the experience of it can offer a kind of psychological completion. This takes the form of aesthetic empathy—a mode of identification with the artist's way of seeing and representing visual possibilities of space-occupancy. For us as social beings, the ways in which other people find meaning in the world is something fascinating. Of course, others might simply tell us what aspects of the spatial world interest them or move them, or how we ought to see them, but no matter how detailed the description, we cannot literally see as they do. In the case of pictorial art, however, the selection of content and the style in which it is rendered allow us to share the artist's vision to some degree at the level of space itself. He or she offers a way of seeing—of interpreting and evaluating the visible world—which we can share or turn away from as we please.

Here, our social relation to the artist is based on freedom rather than beset by the psychological pressures that characterize our normal direct relations with other people. Such empathy is, in logical terms, disinterested, because in order to identify with the aesthetic interpretation of the world presented through the work, we do not need the artist to be physically present. Neither do we need to be aware of empirical facts about the circumstances of the artist's life or his or her broader opinions concerning the world. Of course, we may well know a great deal about the artist, and such knowledge may enhance or inhibit our pleasure. But the point is that we do not have to have it in order to identify with the picture's style of making-visible. Pictorial beauty completes us, by placing artist and audience in a free and mutually beneficial relationship at the level of space.

There is an important corollary to this. We can only understand who and what we are through comparison and contrast with other human beings. In seeing how a picture discloses space-occupying things, we are not only imaginatively absorbed by the artist's style; we also learn things about our own possibilities and/or limitations. Aesthetic empathy through pictures, therefore, facilitates psychological completion in personal as well as social terms.

The general notion of pictorial beauty just described is really a general one. It describes what is involved when we enjoy pictures as art per se. However, it can be qualified further in terms of important subvarieties. The aesthetic transcendence described earlier is an effect of some of these, arising when a work's pictorial beauty actively plays off against our sense of finite limitations. In such cases, we identify not only with the artist's making-visible but also with the way in which it symbolically releases us from finite limitations and, in some circumstances, evokes a sense of the divine. We empathize, in other words, with the artist's positioning of humanity in a more cosmic scheme of things.

This offers a completion of the self that is both aesthetic and metaphysical. By taking us symbolically beyond the limits of finitude, such transcendence provides psychological compensation for our otherwise helpless immersion in the flow of things coming to be and passing away. We are able to possess ourselves. This completion arises from some of the aforementioned subvarieties of pictorial beauty. These are, specifically, "ideal beauty" and what I shall call "metaphysical" and "holistic beauty." It can also arise when the artist's style engages with phenomena or meanings that in some way exceed the scope of our perceptual or imaginative capacities. In this case, we move from the beautiful to the sublime. The sublime operates with pictorial beauty's basic structures of making-visible but in an extreme form—where the relation between the pictorial unity and its suggested illusionistic content involves reference to overwhelming phenomena. In experiences of both the beautiful and the sublime, it is sometimes possible to feel related to a divine presence. Whether this is genuine revelation or exhilarating fantasy is, of course, dependent on the viewpoint of the individual.

The beautiful, the sublime, and evocations of the divine have not been central to theories of pictorial art since 1945—though they have often arisen in discussions of Barnett Newman and Mark Rothko. Jean-François Lyotard has also linked the sublime, in particular, to central aspects of postmodern culture and certain forms of high modernist art, but his approach is extremely schematic and raises severe difficulties that I have addressed elsewhere.[8] And when notions akin to aesthetic transcendence have been considered more generally in earlier philosophy—for example, Kant's notion of aesthetic ideas or Hegel's and Schopenhauer's aesthetics of the visual arts—they have tended to be tied too closely to the problematic metaphysics of those great idealist systems. (Indeed, while Hegel and Schopenhauer are attentive to some distinctive features of pictorial art, they tend to overlook those features that are central to my own account.)[9]

In this book, then, I argue that pictorial art completes us psychologically through its distinctive ways of being beautiful and sublime and of evoking the divine. However, before describing the book's content in more detail, it is worth mentioning, briefly, some other recent treatments of its main concepts. Mary Mothersill's *Beauty Restored* (1984) makes a good case for beauty as a general aesthetic fundamental, and Nick Zangwill (2001) has offered a sustained discussion of the statements we make and beliefs we hold about the beautiful.[10] Jennifer A. McMahon's excellent *Aesthetics and Material Beauty* (2007) develops an account of the general relation between art and beauty that is one of only a few to combine intellectual rigor with keen acuity in discussing particular works of art. Elaine Scarry's *On Beauty and Being Just* (1999) effectively counters some of the politically driven criticisms of beauty that were influential in the 1980s and 1990s. More important, it sees beauty in a broader perspective vis-à-vis its humanizing potential, an insight shared by the present work. Alexander Nehamas' *Only a Promise of Happiness* is an interesting book that offers some interesting ideas—especially in relation to the appreciation of late nineteenth-century French painting. However, it does not consider the cognitive basis of beauty and is, in many respects, more a book of philosophically informed art criticism than a philosophical work. Arthur Pontynen's *For the Love of Beauty* is a polemical work that illuminates problems arising from the widespread dogmatic relativism that blights much contemporary thinking about the arts. One of the strengths of this book is a willingness to formulate a transcultural approach to beauty and cognate normative terms. However, for this to have the impact it deserves, Pontynen's insights need more robust philosophical justification and less dogmatic, religious-based assertion.[11]

As for the sublime, there have been a surprisingly large number of books on the topic since the 1980s. Robert Clewis has discussed the relation between Kant's theory of the sublime and his approach to freedom. Clewis' book is particularly strong in developing an account of the sublime that points toward a correlated notion of respect for nature.[12] Kirk Pillow's study of sublime understanding is a sophisticated work that expounds Kant's and Hegel's theories of the sublime and critically revises and develops them in very searching ways.[13] More recently, Emily Brady has written an important book on the sublime that is wide-ranging in both historical and conceptual terms.[14] There are also two collections, one edited by Simon Morley and the other by Luke White and Claire Pajaczkowska, as well as a volume by Roald Hoffman and Iain Boyd Whyte that explores the sublime across the realms of both art and science.[15]

Most of the aforementioned studies of the beautiful and the sublime deal with visual material, including pictures. But they are far from my own approach in that none of them share the main focus of the present text—namely, the unique ways in which the making of pictures relates to the beautiful and the sublime. Similar limitations apply in relation to the rich contemporary literature on the relation between art and the divine. Richard Harries and Richard Viladesau, among many others, have written relevant works on theological aesthetics, without identifying the distinctive character of pictorial art's contribution.[16] T. J. Gorringe's *Earthly Visions* is different: it has a specifically visual orientation and sensitively interprets a wide range of material. Gorringe says that "what I hope to have shown is the way in which some of the greatest secular art of the past four hundred years can be understood to speak of the presence and reality of God in ways which do not compromise its integrity."[17] More specifically, he affirms that painting "invites us to reflect more deeply on the mystery of existence. It speaks obliquely, and through images, as do parables."[18]

Gorringe is right. Some pictures can indeed be parables of religious meaning, but while this can lead to profound insights, it is not philosophically compelling. Indeed, all the religiously oriented works I have just mentioned (with the partial exception of Gorringe himself) tend somewhat to preach to the converted, or at least to the sympathetic. Someone who is neither converted nor sympathetic will, accordingly, very likely dismiss the religious significance of pictorial art out of hand.

My own approach, in contrast, tries to first establish the relation between pictorial art and aesthetic transcendence on independent metaphysical grounds before raising the question of religious significance. This strategy emphasizes the specific ontologies of visibility that characterize different modes of pictorial art. Through this, I am able to clarify what it is about pictorial art that enables it to have possible religious significance as well as aesthetic meaning. Jean-Luc Marion has also taken some important steps in this direction, but his approach raises far more difficulties than it solves (as will be shown in detail in Chapter 6).[19] In this book, then, I adopt a complex method. It is a postanalytic phenomenology that addresses the beautiful, the sublime, and the divine in pictorial art through close descriptions of the works themselves and through the analysis of relevant theories.

Questions of method aside, the layout of the book is as follows. Chapter 1 investigates the history and philosophy of ideal beauty in Plato, Plotinus, Alberti, Schopenhauer, and then (in much more detail) Sir Joshua Reynolds. By critically developing ideas from Reynolds, in particular, I formulate a theory of ideal beauty as the aesthetic presentation of geometric immanence and the concrete universal. I also show how the notion is still relevant, through discussions of Malevich's late figurative work and Ian Hamilton Finlay's postmodern classicism.

In Chapter 2, another form of aesthetic transcendence in pictorial art is identified, which I call "metaphysical beauty." This has an intimate relation to the ontology of pictorial art—especially linear perspective—and involves an eternalization of our perception of the present and of the systematic structure of spatial recession. I argue that such beauty is in effect the pictorial expression of what might be called the "sensuous divine."

The next chapters consider the sublime. Chapter 3 presents a reconstructed and extended version of Kant's theory, with a new variation that I call the "iconographical sublime." This reconstruction is then explored as the basis for a distinctively pictorial conception of the Kantian sublime. Particular attention is paid to work by the contemporary artist Bracha Lichtenberg Ettinger. Chapter 4 considers the sublime in relation to a tendency in abstract art. It begins with a theory that shows such art to be allusively rather than illusionistically pictorial. The theory is then used to explore the notion of what I call the "mystical sublime" in relation to abstract works, most notably Barnett Newman's Stations of the Cross series and Mark Rothko's Seagram mural project. Specifically, I explain how the mystical sublime in their work can be read in alternative ways—existential, monistic, and theistic.

In Chapter 5, I point out the sense in which art has reached its limits and then consider a creative possibility that crosses photocollage with the compositional strategies of abstract painting and can be developed further through digital imagery. I argue that this idiom is a distinctive variant of the aesthetically transcendent holistic beauty found in painting.

Throughout the book, I show in passing how secular approaches to aesthetic transcendence can also be supplemented—if one is so inclined—by religious interpretations. In the final two chapters, I address the religious dimension of pictorial art in more specific terms. Chapter 6 is a detailed analysis of Jean-Luc Marion's theology of painting. I identify some strengths but argue that the theory has serious deficiencies all along the way—especially in terms of Marion's privileging of the icon and his inadequate notions of art and the aesthetic. The final chapter, Chapter 7, offers an alternative approach to the theology of pictorial art, arguing that it is only with the advent of self-consciousness that a temporal horizon of past, present, future, and possibility comes to exist in the universe. This horizon is made concrete in spatial terms through the making of pictorial art. I argue further that these metaphysical/artistic structures are of religious significance if interpreted in the context of faith. Last of all, I consider (albeit briefly) the general significance of beauty and sublimity in relation to the divine.

# 1  IDEAL BEAUTY AND CLASSIC ART

*A Philosophical Vindication*

## Introduction

When Giotto was born, a painter was generally regarded as a craftsman. Less than two hundred and fifty years later, Charles V, the Holy Roman emperor, not only visited Titian's studio but picked up the artist's brush for him after he had dropped it. The change of status revealed in this anecdote is in no small way concerned with the role of ideal beauty in giving painting the highest cultural legitimation. The origins of ideal beauty—in both practice and theory—are found in classical antiquity. It is hardly surprising, then, that the notion of "classic art," as such, is usually identified with visual practices that draw in some way on classical antiquity's exemplifications of ideal beauty.

## I

In the *Republic*, Plato holds that the only way one can assess the excellence, the beauty, or the rightness of an implement, living thing, or action is by reference to "the use for which it was made, by man or by nature" (601d).[1] It is this that makes art such a problematic notion for Plato. In his philosophy, art's essence is mimetic. But mimesis, in his terms, involves the copying of sensory things and states of affairs. These, however, are themselves only the earthly appearances of the relevant Forms. Hence, the product of artistic mimesis is a copy of a copy and thus twice removed from the authentically real.[2]

On these terms, even if art achieves beauty, the use that is its basis tends to distract us from the contemplation of truth. While Plato is officially dismissive of art's focus on appearance, he nevertheless has an interesting understanding of what its beauty involves. In the *Republic*, for example, he resorts to painting as an analogy in explaining how philosophers should create a legal constitution. The first stage is like a "painting-board" that is wiped clean. In the next stage,

> by selecting behaviour patterns and blending them, they'll produce a composite human likeness, taking as their reference point that quality which Homer . . . called "godly" and "godlike" in its human manifestation. . . . And I suppose they'd rub bits out and paint them in again, until they've done all they can to create human characters which stand the best chance of meeting the gods' approval. (501b–c)[3]

Socrates' interlocutor Adeimantus then observes that this "should be a very beautiful painting" (501c).[4] In all these remarks it is clear that, whatever his reservations about the mimetic outcome of painting, its beauty in realizing this goal involves a selective intervention on the appearances it deals with. It involves idealization.

If Plato does not consider the full implications of this, his great follower Plotinus does, by way of a sculptural example:

> Suppose two blocks of stone lying side by side: one is unpatterned, quite untouched by art; the other has been minutely wrought by the craftsman's hands into some statue of God or man, . . . or if a human being, not a portrait but a creation in which the sculptor's art has concentrated all loveliness. Now it must be seen that the stone thus brought under the artist's hand to the beauty of form is beautiful not as stone—for so the crude block would be as pleasant—but in virtue of the Form or Idea introduced by the art. (5.8.1)[5]

Plotinus draws a vital conclusion from this, specifically, that the arts "give no bare reproduction of the thing seen but go back to the Reason-Principles from which Nature itself derives, and, furthermore . . . much of their work is all their own; they are holders of beauty and add where nature is lacking" (5.8.1).[6] This is a key step forward. The artist's selective intervention on appearance is not just a creating of composite appearances; it strives to remedy defects in appearance through being based on the artist's idea of reality. Plotinus' approach thus resolves some inconsistencies in Plato. The artist's idea is something that nature is made to answer to, through the use of natural materials transformed into a new existent.

By transforming nature into the appearance of an idea, the artist exemplifies the metaphysical dynamic that is at the core of all things. This involves returning the soul—through contemplation and appropriate sorts of action—to the levels of being that sustain it. And while art is not for Plotinus the highest mode of beauty, its great merit is to transform brute matter into the overt embodiment of an idea. Indeed, as we have seen, this is far more than an image or copy. It arises from a forming principle that, through its selectivity, improves the appearance of that which it represents and indicates that there is more to it than mere appearance. The artist's treatment idealizes how the relevant Form appears. By making the appearance beautiful, he or she facilitates the soul's contemplation of that which is higher than nature. The soul is helped to return to its metaphysical sources. Overlooking the meanings of this in the immediate Plotinian context, the key general point is that—by linking art to the idealization of appearance—Plotinus has qualified the Greek notion of beauty in a decisive way. He has identified ideal beauty as basic to art. The beauty of art is based on both creating and improving appearance rather than copying it.

Interestingly, key aspects of the Greek tradition of ideal beauty are found in Alberti's important work *On Painting*. In book 3, for example, we are told that "excellent parts should all be selected from the most beautiful bodies, and every effort must be made to perceive, understand and express beauty."[7] He goes on to note—with the highest approval—a strategy employed by the Greek artist Zeuxis. In Alberti's words, "because he believed that all the things he desired to achieve beauty not only could not be found through his own intuition, but were not to be discovered even in Nature in one body alone, he chose from all the youth of the city five outstandingly beautiful girls that he might represent in his painting whatever feature of feminine beauty was most praiseworthy in each of them."[8]

In these remarks, Alberti is identifying beauty with the outcome of a selective, idealizing process based on the study of relevant phenomena. Centuries later Schopenhauer claimed that the capacity to recognize such beauty involved a priori criteria. In his words:

> We all recognize human beauty when we see it, but in the genuine artist this takes place with such clearness that he shows it as he has never seen it, and in his nature he surpasses nature. . . . He, so to speak, understands nature's *half-spoken words*. . . . Only by virtue of such anticipation also is it possible for us to recognize the beautiful where nature has actually succeeded in the particular case. This anticipation is the *Ideal*; it is the Idea in so far as it is known *a priori*,

or at any rate half-known; and it becomes practical for art by accommodating or supplementing what is given *a posteriori* through nature.[9]

On these terms, we all have a priori knowledge of the Forms of things and beauty so that we can recognize them when they appear. The artist, however, is gifted beyond this, insofar as he or she can complete what nature only suggests. This is possible through the clarity with which he or she comprehends the Form or Idea of natural things. Nature only provides material instances of such Forms, but the artist can discern their essence.

The kind of Platonist insight that Schopenhauer assigns to the artist has a certain naivety. For what the artist does is surely not the translation of some essential image from mind to canvas; it is articulated primarily in terms of his or her pictorial imagination—which is bound up as much (if not more) with the character of the relevant medium.

It is interesting that before Schopenhauer there was a champion of ideal beauty in visual art who offers a statement of it in philosophically quite sophisticated terms, namely, Joshua Reynolds, in his *Discourses on Art*. These didactic works are a collection of his annual presidential addresses to the Royal Academy between 1769 and 1790 (inclusive). Far from being of merely localized historical interest, Reynolds' *Discourses* condense and give systematic justification to the idea of a necessary link between the "grand style" in art and ideal form. He makes the kind of connection between handling the medium and achieving the ideal that Schopenhauer neglects. Moreover, his ideas are a very significant development of the points made by Plato, Plotinus, and Alberti concerning the importance of selectiveness in how the artist articulates form.

## II

The most straightforward aspect of Reynolds' approach is his insistent practical advice. All artists should acquire a basic training in drawing, coloring, and composition and in particular should pay close attention to drawing from life. At the heart of this general orientation, however, a more specific (and interesting) strategy should also be in play, which Reynolds describes as "the accumulation of materials." It is based on copying the works of the great masters—not, it should be added, in slavish terms but in a highly selective way based on a deep knowledge of tradition. The artist's task is to identify and learn from those stylistic factors that are the particular strengths of individual artists, for example, Michelangelo for design, Titian for color, and Ludovico Carracci for a balance of the two.

Reynolds' emphasis on selective interpretation is, of course, at great odds with those theories of artistic creativity that stress the importance of genius. For him, genius is more an achievement of rational mind than it is of inspiration. As he puts it, "invention, strictly speaking, is little more than a new combination of those images which have been previously gathered and deposited in the memory: nothing can come of nothing: he, who has laid up no materials, can produce no combinations."[10] The idea that rational study is at the basis of artistic achievement is one that—as we saw earlier—is already familiar from Alberti's writings and the work of many other theorists. What is distinctive to Reynolds' formulation is his grounding of it in an empiricist theory of perception and knowledge. Before looking at this in detail, however, it is important to comprehend the positive outcome of the selective "accumulation of materials"; such an outcome will be shown to be the very foundation of the grand style.

Everything focuses on a metaphysical claim. Reynolds holds—with the authority of the classical tradition—that "all the arts receive their perfection from an Ideal beauty, superior to what is to be found in individual nature."[11] He explains this in more detail as follows:

> All the objects which are exhibited to our view by nature, upon close examination will be found to have their blemishes and defects. The most beautiful forms have something about them like weakness, minuteness or perfection. It must be an eye long used to the contemplation and comparison of these forms; and which, by long habit of observing what any set of objects of the same kind have in common, has acquired the power of discerning what each wants in particular. This long laborious comparison should be the first study of the painter, who aims at the greatest style.[12]

This strategy, of course, broadly parallels the selective procedure involved in the accumulation of materials. That general idea which the artist has developed through the study of the Old Masters is here used as an analytic tool in relation to phenomena per se. Reynolds next describes its application by the artist:

> His eye being enabled to distinguish the accidental deficiencies, excrescences, and deformities of things, from their general figures, he makes out an abstract idea of their forms more perfect than any one original; and what may seem a paradox, he learns to design naturally by drawing his figures unlike to any one object. This idea of the perfect state of nature, which the Artist calls the Ideal beauty, is the great leading principle by which works of genius are conducted.[13]

Reynolds' doctrine of ideal beauty also moves in a further and more complex direction to encompass ideality of pictorial content as well as form. He holds, for example, that to attain the grand style, the artist must strip his work of contemporary cultural caprices and fashions so as to engage with factors that are of transcultural and transhistorical significance. Such factors take two basic forms. The first is the right kind of universally significant narrative subject matter and the adoption of a morally and aesthetically decorous way of presenting it. In Reynolds' words: "There is a nobleness of conception, which goes beyond any thing in the mere exhibition even of perfect form; there is an art of animating and dignifying the figures with intellectual grandeur, of impressing the appearance of philosophick wisdom, or heroic virtue."[14]

In order to achieve such a presentation, considerable artistic license may be involved. Reynolds notes that although historical figures such as St. Paul and Alexander the Great were of unimpressive physical stature, in his cartoons Raphael represents them in a "poetical" manner, and he is to be applauded for it. What is especially interesting are the grounds on which Reynolds justifies poetic license in this context:

> A painter must compensate the natural deficiencies of his art. He has but one sentence to utter, but one moment to exhibit. He cannot, like the poet or historian, exhibit veneration for the character of the hero or saint he represents. . . . The Painter has no other means of giving an idea of the dignity of mind, but by that external appearance which grandeur of thought does generally, though not always, impress upon the countenance; and by that correspondence of figure to sentiment and situation, which all men wish, but cannot commend.[15]

In these remarks Reynolds underlines a key point of contrast between painting and literary art forms (a contrast, indeed, soon to be made much of by Lessing): that the latter are founded on temporal realization. In literary works a subject can be described at length through time, whereas in painting the subject is rendered through a single appearance or set of aspects with a fixed relation to the viewer. It is the constraints of the medium itself, therefore, that warrant the idealization of content in the sense described earlier. To do full justice to the heroic stature of the subject, narrative elements must be harmonized with properties that are inherent to the nature of the medium itself.

This process of idealization also involves a specific general attitude toward elements of pictorial content. Put briefly, it requires that the artist avoid stylistic touches that emphasize the particularity of the rendered subject. Such things as wild gestures or exaggerated facial expressions, as well as attentiveness to exact details of textures or drapery, are for Reynolds factors that inhibit the presentation of ideal beauty—even though they may not, in literal terms, be blemishes or imperfections. Similar considerations even hold for him in relation to details of color. All in all, the parts of a painting—whatever closeness they may bear to the "truth" of surface appearances—must be entirely subordinate to the overall principle of design and grouping. In Reynolds' words: "The general idea constitutes real excellence. All smaller things, however perfect in their way, are to be sacrificed without mercy to the greater."[16] Indeed, "if deceiving the eye were the only business of the art, there is no doubt . . . but the more minute painter would be apt to succeed: but it is not the eye, it is the mind, which the painter of genius desires to address."[17]

This distinction between art that merely addresses the senses and art that can engage the mind is, for Reynolds, the basis of a hierarchical conception of pictorial art, ranging from history painting—themes from classical culture, themes from scripture, heroic historical events (sacred or profane), and courtly scenes—through (in descending order of intellectual worth) landscapes, genre painting, portraits, and still lifes. Within this hierarchy, it is only the history painter who offers an authentic embodiment of the grand style. Such a painter is a figure of the highest intellectual stature, whose works are on a par with philosophy and indeed historical writing, as well as the literary arts.

III

Reynolds' conception of ideal beauty is remarkably sophisticated. In holding that there is one ideal form for each individual species, he is an inheritor of the classical tradition of philosophy. However, the real emphasis in his account falls on such forms not as transcendent ontological entities but rather as mental formulations, achieved by means of processes of abstraction. In effect, Reynolds reinterprets the ideal on the analogy of eighteenth-century empiricist approaches to mind and perception, in particular, the Lockean notion of "general ideas."[18] It is the grand style's orientation toward this notion that ratifies it as an aesthetic activity with a value beyond the mere pleasure of the senses.

This analogy is problematic, but in rather complex and interesting ways. At first sight it appears widely off the mark, if only by virtue of the fact that the notion of general ideas in Locke and others is a fundamental feature of basic cognitive activity and does not characterize philosophical thought alone.

If Reynolds' analogy were apt, in other words, it would point more toward the commonplace significance of the ideal rather than toward some elevated intellectual status. Against this, Reynolds might reply that the analogy with elevated thought is nonetheless appropriate because the painter does not simply make cognitive discriminations but does so on the basis of a complex technical education, as well as, more significantly, a way of seeing informed by the "accumulation of materials," that is, the selective interpretation of tradition noted earlier. The grand style's ideal beauty offers a more complete comprehension of visual forms and narratives than does ordinary perception or description.

At this point, however, we must consider a deeper problem. To his credit, Reynolds anticipates the following potential objection: "in every particular species there are various central forms, which are separate and distinct from each other, and yet are undeniably beautiful; that in the human figure, for instance, the beauty of Hercules is one, of the Gladiator another; which makes so many different ideas of beauty."[19] In answer to this, Reynolds affirms that these are ideals pertaining to specific classes within a species. However, "perfect beauty in any species must combine all the characters which are beautiful in that species. It cannot consist in any one to the exclusion of the rest: no one, therefore, must be predominant, that no one may be deficient."[20] Ideal beauty, in other words, must be derived through abstraction from that of the various classes which constitute the species in question.

But we must ask what this process of abstraction actually amounts to. Locke notes that in order to form the general idea of "man," young children do not posit something other than a particular man "but only leave out of the complex idea they had of Peter and James, Mary and Jane, that which is peculiar to each, and retain that which is common to all."[21] Such a notion of abstraction is very close to that of Reynolds. In relation to Locke, however, Berkeley makes the following critical observation:

> I can imagine a man with two heads, or the upper part of a man joined to the body of a horse. I can consider that hand, the eye, the nose, each by itself abstracted or separated from the rest of the body. But then whatever eye or hand I imagine, it must have some particular shape and color. Likewise the idea of a man that I frame to myself; must be either of a white, or a black, or a tawny, a straight or a crooked, a tall, or a low, or a middle-sized man. I cannot by any effort conceive the abstract idea above described [by Locke].[22]

Given the schematic and elusive character of mental images per se, Berkeley's invocation of particularity here is not wholly decisive. If, however, like Reynolds, one seeks to present a general idea in concrete visual terms (i.e., through painting), then Berkeley's objection has great force. One cannot present a visual instantiation of ideal beauty except through a particular instance of the species in question. There is, of course, a sense in which an artist can idealize his or her subject matter, by removing blemishes or rectifying disproportions, but this falls far short of the positive criterion of ideality that Reynolds is advocating. Indeed, in the final analysis, how one characterizes his notion of ideal beauty will, in terms of its positive content, be highly arbitrary. As a positive notion, the ideal is simply too broad to be concretely exemplified in a definite form. Any definiteness we give to it will be stipulative.

The problem is exacerbated. Reynolds sees a vast range of artists—even encompassing the likes of Rubens and Rembrandt—as practitioners of ideal beauty. In effect, all the great artists (except those who devote themselves to still life) are artists in the grand style. But this makes the question of assigning a positive content to ideal beauty even more problematic. How could artists so different from one another all be abstracting toward the features that are essential to the subject they are representing? What we find in their works are recognizable kinds of things, mainly free of blemishes and not in ungainly proportion, but over and above this they are different from one another and often quite radically so. It would seem to be impossible to give any positive content to what ideal beauty involves.

There are many other significant problems with Reynolds' approach. Central among these is his ill-advised attempt to devise a hierarchy of genres on the basis of orientation toward the particular. This hierarchical scale, as already mentioned, involves history painting at the top and still life's lowly pleasure in visual detail at the bottom. The fundamental weakness of this idea is its complete insensitivity to the metaphorical dimension of pictorial art. I do not simply mean the capacity for paintings (including still lifes) to carry allegorical meaning; rather, the treatment of detail and particularity can have this significance in itself. Zurbaran's still lifes, for example, often depict ceramic surfaces with such luminous but controlled intensity as to invoke the sheer wonder of quiddity and material being. And in cruder terms, one might equally well (in Ruskinian mood) regard attention to detail in all the genres as being a celebration of the sensuous divine as much as a "feast for the eye" as such. One can posit other interpretations of the genres that allow painting a "lofty" significance without introducing a hierarchical dimension.

A contextualist approach to art history and theory might question whether the critical analysis I have offered is even worth undertaking, since one knows at the outset that "it will all end in tears" simply by virtue of Reynolds' manifest position in a white, male, racist, patriarchal, middle-class network of eighteenth-century power relations. What is needed, on this contextualist view, is a genealogy that can clarify Reynolds' relation to this network.[23] And in truth a genealogical analysis of this kind can be of interest—but not if it attempts to reduce Reynolds' theory to no more than a position in a broader network of power relations. The advantage of my approach is that it reveals the depth, complexity, and original character of his strategy. Whatever shortcomings Reynolds' theory may have, it pushes us in the direction of a deeper meaning to art than that of narrative or decorative value.[24] Indeed, the theory can be modified as follows so as to be of continuing use.

## IV

In order to justify ideal beauty in the visual arts, it will be useful first of all to briefly consider artistic styles that are not ideal in orientation. Terms such as "realism" and "naturalism," for example, pick out works that tend to focus on specific characteristics of concrete existing individuals, be they humans, animals, or factors in a landscape. Representations of this kind often invite us to draw more general moral or political conclusions, but the means to this is the insistent particularity of what is represented.

More painterly styles—in the tradition of Rubens, or those of figures such as Delacroix, Gauguin, and Van Gogh and the many varieties of twentieth-century expressionism—also place great stylistic emphasis on the individual and particular character of what is represented. We can recognize that this is a picture of such-and-such a kind of thing, person, or state of affairs, but the emphasis is on the individual represented and the way in which the relevant configuration of defining properties is concretely realized in this distinctive individual. This can even be true of schematic works. One would imagine that these would favor general features, but in an artist such as Raoul Dufy, simple schematic means are used to achieve intense and "busy" evocations of visual particulars rather than visual kinds. Indeed, the existence of cartoon and caricature is based on schematic representation that evokes quite specific individuals (real or merely imagined) in the most insistent terms.

The art of ideal beauty has an entirely different emphasis from these stylistic tendencies. For reasons outlined in Section II, Reynolds' cognitivist theory cannot explain or justify the ideal. That being said, however, there are some workable strands of argument that can be refounded and supplemented. First, we will recall Reynolds' position on the removal of blemishes and imperfections. The meaning of "blemishes" is straightforward; that of "imperfections" is based on the fact that particular members of a species may have parts—either individually or in relation to one another and/or the whole—that are disproportionate or disfigured. The criterion of this is how the part or parts in question deviate from some physical norm (in terms of appearance and constitution) that is characteristic of the species in question. As we have seen, Reynolds insisted on ideal form being linked to the general characteristics of species, but this goes further than required and creates the problems noted earlier. One should be content, rather, to suppose that there are norms of appearance for genuses or classes within species or kinds, rather for the species and kinds as such.

What counts as a norm, of course, is not at all straightforward and may involve some element of openness. Inevitably questions of cultural location will play a key role. The norm for an ideal man or woman, for example, will mainly be determined by preferences within a culture or geographical location. However, this is not simply a case of preference. The ideal form is one that stands out from others and the grounds of whose difference from the more mundane examples can be pointed out through argument and analysis in relation to the particular case. And this can be transcultural. Given two very different examples of the ideal from different cultures, one can give reasons why one is to be preferred to the other by considering factors having to do with symmetry and proportion.

Notwithstanding all this, being properly configured in relation to the relevant norm of appearance is only a necessary condition of ideal beauty in art. There are other important features that allow the positive character of such beauty to be explained in yet more specific terms. Reynolds himself offers at least one important clue concerning this. We will recall how in "accumulating materials" the artist must look to the achievements of the great masters and study the pictorial features that are the special strength of the master in question. Here Reynolds acknowledges that whatever the philosophical basis of the grand style, its exemplars have their own individual stylistic perspectives on it. Titian and the Venetians are especially strong on color, Michelangelo on composition, and so on.

What this means is that the grand style is given vitality not only through its orientation toward the ideal as such but to individual stylistic distinctiveness and emphases in how this is realized. If a painter has an individual style, this means that the symmetry and proportions and other compositional elements in the work must not only be free from blemishes and imperfections and properly proportioned, but must be so in a nonformulaic and visually interesting way. The achievement of individual style vis-à-vis the ideal means that its appearance also has an element of freedom. The general content is not forced upon the particular representation; rather, the two aspects enable one another.

This notion of ideal beauty can now be linked to a second strand of argument from Reynolds. As well as the ideal being a feature of forms, he also holds that it applies to narrative content and the characterization of individual persons as well. Generalizing, one might say that content is idealized when it presents clearly defined, physically robust, psychologically and/or morally strong individuals, involved in psychologically and/or morally significant narratives. And in the case of landscape or still life, parallel examples might center on a clarity of form that carries the suggestion of allegorical meanings beyond mere phenomenal presence.

Reynolds clearly regarded this normative character as necessary to every instance of the ideal, but it is not. For one can have works that are ideal in form but have a licentious and/or decadent content; equally, one can have works with strong moral power rendered in painterly or expressionist style rather than one that is formally ideal. At best, we can say that ideality of narrative or of character is frequently found in works that have ideal beauty of form and it is the latter that is decisive.

In Section II we saw how Reynolds applies ideal beauty to an impossibly wide range of artists. This can be narrowed down by means of a further criterion that allows the ideal to be identified even more specifically, which I shall call "geometrical immanence." It is found in pictorial art whose ideality declares more-basic three-dimensional geometric forms (usually in some combination, or even irregularly varied) such as spheres, cones, pyramids, cubes, cylinders, ovoids, and rectangular and triangular prisms, as well as the faces, edges, vertices, and partial segments of such forms. These structures are the basis of perceptual constancies. By reference to them we both recognize different appearances as being of the same object and recognize them as characteristics of an individual kind; or to put it in ontological terms, geometric structure sustains the identity of the particular as particular and its identity as a particular of this specific kind. This is where pictorial art intersects most closely with those Platonic Forms that are spatial in character.

Forms of this sort, it should be emphasized, are metaphysically as well as epistemologically fundamental. Space-occupancy is the main criterion of something existing and is central to the notion of primary qualities. Geometric structures are basic elements from which the fabric of spatial appearance itself is composed. Indeed, insofar as we exist as embodied agents in a field of action, it is through negotiating the three-dimensional spatial structures just described. They are the existential signature of spatial structure in things and relations as experienced. As such, they have a familiarity and intimacy that is elided when we studied them simply in the context of geometry. Ideal art, in contrast, restores geometric structure to the level of lived experience and makes it harmonious both with norms of appearance and with the particulars that instantiate such appearance. Such art declares space in its structural fullness and allows it to be experienced in aesthetic terms—as a contemplative pleasure.

Religious believers may go even further and find an element of divine revelation within the aesthetic. For while we can explain individual geometric structures and their relations to one another, we cannot explain why space should have just these specific geometric "signatures." Space could, in principle, have come to exist with a different structure, but for us it exists in just the way it does. For religious believers, this must be for a reason. The signatures may themselves, accordingly, be signs of a logic of world-ordering that is divinely ordained. The immanent geometric structures are, as it were, God's thinking of space so as to provide physical conditions that enable the evolution and survival of rational embodied subjects. Insofar as the artist works with these very same structures, therefore, his or her creative powers follow in the shadow of God's creativity. Of course, whether or not one finds and accepts this "sign" is a question of faith. But it is at least a possibility that those of religious disposition may consider.

It might be objected that geometric immanence can be a strong feature of art other than the ideal; Van Gogh's painting of Gauguin's chair at Arles, for example, has such an emphasis. But while all three-dimensional items will have geometric form (insofar as they are three-dimensional), what is decisive—if they do emphasize it—is *how* it is thus disclosed. In many cases (and this is especially true of Van Gogh's painting) the relevant features emphasize the particular character of the item or state of affairs being represented, or accentuate its expressive or decorative features. In ideal beauty, in contrast, particular features of color and texture are constrained so as to allow geometric immanence to emerge in a way that has visual equality with these more particular features.

On the basis of the Reynoldsian criteria, together with geometric immanence, a metaphysical criterion of the ideal may thus be established. It offers a philosophical justification of ideal beauty in visual art on grounds other than those offered by Reynolds—while still including those strands of his arguments that are viable. This justification centers on the "concrete universal"—a term that is derived from the Hegelian tradition but will not be interpreted here with particular reference to Hegel. According to this view, the relation between a phenomenal concept and its instances is one of reciprocal dependence. The phenomenal concept involves a unified configuration of properties that defines a class of sensible particulars. However, this configuration exists only through being embodied in such particulars: they get their general kind-character from it, and it becomes physically real through them. In other words, general terms are not abstracted from their particular instances. One can isolate one or the other of the two aspects through analysis, but ontologically speaking, they are mutually dependent. Our recognition of concepts and particular instances of them is based on comprehending the reciprocal dependence of their relation, rather than inferring one from the other.

The doctrine of geometric immanence is of key importance in the concrete universal. For as already noted, it is the basis of the perceptual constants that enable us to identify different appearances as being of one and the same particular spatial object; at the same time, it is also a necessary basis of the appropriate configuration of spatial shapes and forms that enable us to identify a particular as a spatial object of a specific kind. It is the factor that bonds the reciprocal dependence of particular and universal in any spatial object.

Such reciprocal dependence is basic to concept use and thus to all aspects of human consciousness, but it is not much remarked upon or attended to outside the realm of philosophy. However, it does impinge upon pictorial and sculptural representation. We will recall that ideal beauty in art involves the removal of blemishes and imperfections insofar as the parts of something deviate from the norm. It also involves factors pertaining to symmetry and proportion above and beyond this norm. These factors are enhanced through the individual style in which they are expressed in the particular work—their ideality has a certain freedom of appearance as well. Ideal beauty also involves the affirmation of geometric immanence. Here, in contrast to realist, naturalist, and expressionist art, the harmonious reciprocity between universal and particular is fundamental. Ideal art is the aesthetic affirmation of the concrete universal. The individual features of the work—through the very character of their individuality—draw attention to the more general features of the subject matter, and by so doing, they emphasize the reciprocity between individuality and universality—the concrete universal.

So then, what is the aesthetic "pay-off" from all this? The answer lies in the deeper meaning of ideal beauty's clarification of the reciprocal harmony of individual instance and universal. This meaning centers on the logical transcendence of the universal—its existence in different individuals spread out across a potential infinity of different times and places. Whereas the logically transcendent character of universal terms is normally a mere background feature of their ordinary use, the enjoyment of ideal beauty in art brings this into more active play. We know intuitively that what enables this beauty is a harmony of the individual and the general that is fundamental to knowledge itself.

In the contemplation of such beauty, a sense of wonder arises at the way this structure inhabits innumerable other instances, in other places and times, and is available for contemplation by innumerable other agents. The individual item clarifies the grandeur of generality at the level of the senses or the imagination. This clarification not only centers on the specific individual-universal relation involved but may even involve a sense of the ubiquity of the individual-Form relation per se, in our knowledge of self and world.

Thus, ideal beauty is ennobled appearance—a reciprocity between the individual presentation and its defining universal—that makes the logical transcendence of the universal (and the subject's relation to it) come alive in perception or imagination. Our contemplation is focused on this relation but has, at the same time, a psychological intensity owing to the element of ennobled appearance. The transcendence becomes aesthetic as well as logical; we have the feeling of both the Form and ourselves being here and elsewhere simultaneously. Such an experience is intrinsically rewarding: a felt transcendence of our finite limitations in being tied to the here and now of our immediate presence to objects of perception. Ideal beauty involves a concentration on the particular which cognitively both implodes and explodes upon itself at the same time. We are lifted by the particular's idealized appearance to a more universal level, that of the Form's distribution across different instances, times, places, and conditions of observation.

The question then arises as to which specific art historical tendency is ideally beautiful in the terms just described. In this regard, it is interesting that within the Renaissance, as well as before and after it, there are artists whose orientation toward ideal beauty has a specific kind of purity. It is in reference to the works of these artists that ideal beauty can be made specific in a way that takes us beyond Reynolds' empty generalities. Piero della Francesca, Mantegna, Michelangelo, Poussin, Flaxman, David, Ingres, Gérôme, Leighton, and Poynter, among others, not only favor the idealizing features I have identified in Reynolds but accentuate them in the specific directions outlined above.

The artists in question here satisfy Heinrich Wölfflin's criteria of the classic tendency in art. His criteria emphasize linear features, outlines and the limits of things ("the perception of individual material objects as solid, tangible bodies")[25] expressing forms and their parts through sequences of planes, the organization of space itself in sequential planimetric recession, with forms and narrative in the picture appearing as constrained and/or aligned with the edges of the picture itself.[26]

These features, in concert, allow the beholder to discern a logic in how forms present individually and are composed in relation to one another. Though Wölfflin does not remark upon it, this involves particulars presented through emphases on those primary qualities such as shape, position, and size that sustain particular appearances of the kind of object in question (i.e., geometric immanence). The planimetric and self-contained character of the overall pictorial space serves to accentuate these clarifications rather than create an optical ambiguity of spatial recession.

Now, as Wölfflin himself admits, how these features apply is relative rather than absolute. Whether or not an artist's work is "classic" in his sense depends on with whom one is comparing that artist. However, if one links Wölfflin's criteria to the account of ideal beauty based on the concrete universal, then a recognizable art historical tendency can be identified in more precise terms. All the artists mentioned above—from Piero della Francesco to Poynter (and many more besides)—would be hard to describe in terms that did not involve the concept of ideal beauty explained above. This is not just because many of them favor classic subject matter but because of the way their pictures appear. In other words, ideal beauty should be understood as exemplified mainly by the classical tradition in painting—not only the Old Masters but also others who fit the concrete universal–based criteria that have been enumerated. Let us now consider some examples.

Piero della Francesca's *Baptism of Christ* (1448–1450) (Figure 1) is a work that, in compositional terms, is both complex and simple (without being simplistic). The trees and figures offer strong perpendicular emphases distributed

FIGURE 1. Piero della Francesca, *Baptism of Christ*, 1448–1450. National Gallery, London. Reprinted with permission.

across a shared plane. The limbs and musculature of the exposed arms, legs, and torsi emphasize the body's emergence from complex combinations and segments of more basic ovoid, cylindrical, and spherical forms. Indeed, the perpendicular axes of the human figures are not merely "in" the figures' upright postures; rather, these postures proclaim those axes insistently—a proclamation that Piero emphasizes through its echo in the rigid perpendicularity of the tree trunk, which accentuates the posture and pale coloration of Christ. Through these echoes and juxtapositions, the upright postures not only affirm the vertical axis of the human form but also connote "uprightness" in a more ideal sense of moral resolve.

This feeds, of course, into the narrative content of the painting. Christ, John the Baptist, and the onlookers have individual expressions and poses but are situated in a shared psychological space of solemn regard. They existentially constellate, as it were, around the intensity of Christ's resolve. Christ's countenance clearly envisions his power of redemption and the suffering it involves, but the physical and social setting in which he is presented also underlines the fact that it is the humanity he shares with others (as well as his divine origin) that enables him to offer redemption. The whole work, in other words, is pervaded by an ideal—the authority of Christ the Redeemer and the redemption that he bestows.

The color of the painting also relates to this narrative meaning: it is extremely restrained. In particular, the protagonists' apparel has no significant textures over and above those created by the modest folds of drapery. These folds not only clothe the figures but have a wrinkled character that perhaps alludes to the ultimate withering and death of the body. In fact, throughout the work the human form and its clothing not only are well-balanced between particular detail and general structure, but are so with a kind of visual austerity. Even the angel's robes, while intense in color, are composed of monochrome parts rather than resplendent textures. All in all, these are real individuals in a real physical setting, but in a narrative context whose more universal significance is exemplified through how this reality is presented.

Piero's painting, then, offers a harmonious reciprocity between the ideal and particularity. This same reciprocity can be found in Nicolas Poussin's *A Bacchanalian Revel Before a Term* (1632) (Figure 2), albeit in a contrasting way. Unlike the della Francesca work, this is a highly animated composition, with a crisp momentum from left to right, unfolding through the rhythmically distributed figures. There is no idealization of narrative in moral terms, as the

FIGURE 2. Nicolas Poussin, *A Bacchanalian Revel Before a Term*, 1632. National Gallery, London. Reprinted with permission.

represented scene is one of licentious abandon. Yet there is an exquisite balance between the articulation of flesh and the disposition of the body, on the one hand, and the restrained expression of color (especially in the drapery), on the other. The bodies and flesh are well modeled, while the figures' gestures are meaningful not only as presentations of movement but through being at the same time displays of limbs and torsi in extended elevation (rather than merely being presented frontally). Through this extension, the visual character of the human body as an intersection of various geometric forms—cylinders, spheres, and segments thereof—is declared in a robust yet lyrical way.

The importance of the colored drapery in this work cannot be overstated. It balances individual striations with more general hanging folds, the latter of which are the main source of the work's visual momentum. Poussin's strategy here is assisted by his way of emphasizing shadow. Rather than using it merely to declare the three-dimensional bulk of the drapery, the artist deploys it to accentuate our sense of the drapery's animation as well. This in turn accentuates the display of limbs and torsi in their extended elevations.

Finally, let us consider Lord Leighton's *Captive Andromache* (1888) (Figure 3). Classic art remains a powerful force even into the nineteenth and early

FIGURE 3. Frederic, Lord Leighton, *Captive Andromache*, 1888. Whitworth Gallery, Manchester. Reprinted with permission.

twentieth centuries through the work and influence of figures such as Leighton, Alma-Tadema, Poynter, and Watts in the United Kingdom and Ingres, Delaroche, Gérôme, and Bourgereau in France. The artists in question here in many cases go beyond restraint in how particularity of appearance is rendered. They tend, for example, to present scenes and interiors of a visually opulent character—expressed through lavish attention to architectural detail and settings and to such things as the textures of marble and stone, timbers, wall hangings, statuary, flowers, hair, gowns, and the general attire of the figures.

However, within this "perfumed particularity" there are many individual works that remain closer to the purer classic model, including Leighton's *Captive Andromache*. The work is composed of individuals and groups of figures placed along a foreground and along a central plane, engaged in everyday outdoor domestic activities. There is a subtle visual polyphony suggested by highlights, colors, and the spatial arrangement of bodies and gestures. This polyphony plays around—both converging upon and moving away from—the central figure in the black robe.

At the heart of this visual strategy is a perfect fusion of gesture, color, shadow, and in particular, bodily activity. This activity comprises a range of gestural orientations—standing upright, being seated, reaching down—and finds its most interesting expression in the partial view of a male figure with his arms hung around a staff carried along his shoulders (to the left of center in the foreground plane). Through the disposition of figures and their gestures, Leighton's picture explores geometric immanence—the manifestness of general spatial structures through particular presentations of them—in an especially calibrated way.

And again, this complements the narrative dimension of the work. The black-robed Andromache—Hector of Troy's wife (now enslaved)—waits to fill her jug with water. A woman in yellow to her right (from the viewer's position) struggles with the jug she is carrying. Some of the other figures look on in a casual or indifferent way—but we cannot be sure whether they are looking at Andromache or at the struggling girl. Andromache's personal tragedy is now just one life among many others, a fact acknowledged in the wistful resignation she expresses. She who was once exalted and apart from the life of toil has now been cast into the mundane rhythm of working life—a rhythm embodied in the picture's controlled polyphony.

Ideal art should be identified, then, with the recurrent classic tendency in Western art. This often involves subject matter taken from classical sources, but the decisive criterion of its ideality is the harmonious reciprocity between norm-presenting features, particular details, and at the heart of both of these, geometric immanence. In many works, a normative narrative content is also a feature of the ideal, insofar as is integrated with the other features just described.

Feminist art historians might argue that the approach just taken overlooks the oppressive aspects of classic art, specifically the way much of it offers the female form as an object for the male gaze. However, the criteria proposed here can actually have an opposite and critical significance: they offer a means of distinguishing between mere presentations of the female form for the male gaze and forms where geometric immanence rather than erotic provocation is to the fore.

This same approach can solve a related art historical puzzle, namely, the enduring appeal of Michelangelo's treatment of the nude and in particular his androgynous females, whose erotic accent is (as far as I can tell) fairly minimal. The nudes in question seem to assert themselves as idealizations of the naked human figure; but if that were all they were, they would be failures—highly particular muscle-bound overstatements. But this expression of the ideal also incorporates a high level of imaginatively presented geometric immanence, in terms of overall pose, more particular dispositions of limbs and torsi, facial expression, and musculature. The particularity of the nude harmonizes with the universal in its geometric immanence aspect, with aspiration to the ideal norm playing only a mediating role.

It should be emphasized that in this theory no hierarchical status is assigned to classic art. The grounds of its aesthetic distinctiveness have been described above. But realist, naturalist, and expressionist works have ontological structures of their own that make them aesthetically distinctive in specific respects.[27] Indeed, classic art can degenerate into mere stereotype and lend itself to low-grade application in the fields of advertising and political propaganda.

However, this theory at least explains *why* classicism and ideal beauty in art are aesthetically justified and of recurrent interest. Pictorial art of this kind completes us in psychological terms through offering visual cognition based on aesthetic transcendence. For while all spatial phenomena involve geometric immanence and concrete universality, classic art makes them burst forth from the mundane spatiality in which they are generally contained. Such features can, of course, be described or explained to us, but in classic art we engage with them at the level of space-occupancy itself, as revealed through the picture. Vision and our sense of belonging (physically and psychologically) to the shared spatial world are given a more complete expression through being focused by aesthetic transcendence.

The final question to be addressed concerns the future. It is obvious that classicism and ideal beauty no longer have authority in the field of art practice, having been substantially marginalized since the end of the First World War. Yet this is by no means the end of the matter, for the ideal beauty of classic art has managed some unexpected adaptations. It has played, for example, a very complex role in surrealism and cognate tendencies—most notably in the paintings of Magritte, Dalí, and de Chirico, where classical or quasi-classical statuary and idealized figures are recurring motifs. Here the ideal features are invested with a dreamlike quality through the untoward contexts in which they are represented. The relation between the ideal and the dreamlike, in fact, is an important topic that could be explored in great detail in its own right. For present purposes, however, it will be more useful to consider a couple of less obvious expressions of the ideal.

## V

The first interesting case is that of Malevich's three-quarter portraits of 1932–1935, which are eerily generalized in terms of detail and pose and whose subjects are clothed in a way that alludes to Renaissance fashion without being exactly representative of it. There is a curious, almost simplistic idealization of form and content here that evokes a sense of dignified resistance to the encroachments of social realism. Although the best-known work from this late series by Malevich is his *Self-Portrait* of 1934, I will consider *Girl with a Red Pole* (1932–1933). In this picture, as in all the others in the series, Malevich nominally reaffirms his commitment to abstract art by disguising it within a figurative context. The girl's features and clothing have particular details, but these are explored as a way of emphasizing more basic geometric volumes. Texture is diminished to the vanishing point so that areas of pure color can be modeled as intersecting segments of solid ovoid. The pole that the girl is holding is a thin, horizontal cylinder. It may be a detached pole or one that serves as a rail; whatever the case, the girl's hands inhibit the continuity of its appearance and thus introduce a restrained visual animation into the otherwise still volumes that dominate the center of the painting. A similar effect is achieved through the two leaf-shaped extensions of her headgear. The overall formal effect is of the volumes in the central part of the picture pressurizing and meeting resistance from the horizontal pole. The girl's static appearance is the result of a stasis arising from a balance of visual forces at work in the composition.

This is abstraction in disguise, but it is also much more than that. The deeper suggestion is that the familiar world of three-dimensional objects and creatures actually takes on its character as a result of interactions between more basic forms. In his earlier work, Malevich explored these forms abstractly, as a means of suggesting deeper (spiritual) levels of reality. Here, in effect, he shows that the material reality represented in officially approved figurative idioms is actually derived from something much more fundamental. In this respect, Malevich's strategy is akin to that possible interpretation of geometric immanence mentioned earlier, wherein the geometric signatures of the spatial world may be taken to have a religious significance.

The point is that in Malevich's very late work, classic art's orientation toward the concrete universal is made into something at once overtly metaphysical and political, through a kind of highly focused ideal visual purity. Interestingly, some equally complex transformations can be found in the work of Ian Hamilton Finlay in the last quarter of the twentieth century. Although he occupies an entirely different historical and cultural context from Malevich, Finlay's work was likewise in large part stimulated by a sense of oppression. He felt that in an increasingly consumerized age, culture had lost its sense of piety—its reverence for modes of thinking humanity's place in the cosmos as such. The creation of his garden at Little Sparta in Midlothian, Scotland, can accordingly be seen as an attempt to create a space where piety is restored.

What is remarkable, however, is the complex means whereby this is realized, which extend beyond merely laying out a garden. In exploring the garden, the viewer comes across unexpected and uncanny artifacts: for example, *Apollon Terroriste*, a classical head of Apollo, painted in gold with the work's title inscribed on the forehead. Why Apollo, why a terrorist, and why is the title in French? Well, in a pious age, Apollo can project radiant open sunlight and ride across the sky. But this is an age without piety; accordingly, the god has been driven into the undergrowth, and he has absorbed the sunlight into himself. In this wooded setting, to encounter him is not only to be startled, it is to be threatened. The intense gold of Apollo's head is so strikingly askew from its wooded context as to do violence to our comfortable sense of walking the garden's trail. He is ready to attack the impious world—starting here and now.

The titling of the work in French extends the connotations of violence. In many of Finlay's designed artworks (over and above those in situ at Little Sparta) neoclassical motifs and titles are linked explicitly to figures, events, and ideas from pre-Napoleonic revolutionary France. At that time, through figures such as Jacques-Louis David and Charles Nodier, neoclassicism had become an aesthetic gesture of republican resistance to the ancien régime. It combined all the features I have linked to ideal beauty and the concrete universal and, in so doing, positioned itself as a yearning for visual and moral purification at odds with the old regime's frivolous rococo sensibility. David's dictum sums it up perfectly: "The purpose of the arts is to serve morality and elevate the soul."

Finlay presents neoclassicism as an aesthetic to challenge consumerist mediocrity and impiety through its visual purity and (in his work) thought-provoking character. But when an aesthetic of classical purity is also an expression of a broader ethical and political position, there are consequences. Imperfections have to be eliminated, and fatefully, the notion of imperfection has often been extended to people as well as to forms, which is why so much of Finlay's imagery develops the implications of violence contained in classic art's societal positionings. His controversial use of such things as Nazi SS runes shows a willingness not only to embrace classic art as a continuing creative legacy but to be honest enough to remind us of its destructive potency.

However, while Finlay gazes into the abyss, as it were, the bulk of his work takes us far beyond it. This is because much of it has genuine ideal beauty of a pure, rather than a purificationist, kind. In particular, his work is especially attentive to the phenomenon of geometric immanence, which allows him at times to negotiate the aesthetic and violent potential of classic art even within a single work.

Consider, for example, *Five Finials* (with Peter Coates; 2001). The finials display exceptional restraint in terms of both shape and color while emphasizing spheres, ovoids, and rectangular prisms (Figure 4). Despite differences of size and visual complexity, there is no hierarchy among the finials. But there is a problem with the one on the far right: not only is it in the form of a hand grenade, but its pin and detonation lever are in black and thus entirely incon-

FIGURE 4. Ian Hamilton Finlay, *Five Finials*, 2001. Stone; each 39 × 21 × 21 cm. Nolan Judin Gallery, Berlin. Courtesy the artist's estate and Victoria Miro, London. © The Estate of Ian Hamilton Finlay. Photo: Robert Glowacki.

gruous with the work's other elements. The visual incongruity here suggests, of course, an incongruity in moral terms as well. The hand grenade's form has the potential to be represented in the classic mode; but what a hand grenade is means that something alien to ideal beauty will intrude upon such a representation—the black of the pin and lever emphasize this. They are expressed as alien growths, a potential for violence that may extend itself when ideal beauty is not qualified by the appropriate societal contexts and concerns.

## Conclusion

This leads us finally to the contemporary and future meanings of ideal beauty in classic art. The ideal has been marginalized and will never hold the privileged position it once had. Its intrinsic meaning as the artistic expression of the concrete universal can still be a source of pleasure, but there are now many other competing artistic strategies available—each with its own distinctiveness and worth. As the contrasting examples of Malevich and Ian Hamilton Finlay show, however, societal circumstances can be such as to sometimes favor a reinterpretation of ideal beauty in classic art. The Ideal then takes its place as a recurrent possibility of aesthetic meaning that can be inflected differently under different societal contexts. It may be a minority interest, but one with the capacity to be revived and rearticulated as circumstances demand.

Indeed, the very fact that classic art is immediately recognizable as a tendency whose time of authority has passed invests its anachronistic character with a critical edge. By being so insistently *not* of present origins, it is able to indict and to offer an alternative aesthetic horizon to the dominant aesthetic ideologies of the moment—or, of course, the absence of them. Ideal beauty and classic art now exist as permanent possibilities of critique.

# 2  PICTORIAL ART AND METAPHYSICAL BEAUTY

## Introduction

In the Introduction to this book, it was argued that pictorial beauty extends beyond its basic idiom to modes of aesthetic transcendence centered on the symbolic overcoming of finite limitations. The ideal beauty discussed in Chapter 1 is an example of this transcendence. We turn now to a less familiar case of it, which I call "metaphysical beauty."

## I

The term "picture" is used in many different ways and in relation to many different idioms of visual representation. However (as stated in the Introduction to this book), I follow the usage that takes picturing to be a convention whereby the appearance of some recognizable kind of visual three-dimensional item or state of affairs is created in a virtually two-dimensional plane with the intention of enabling the viewer to recognize the three-dimensional form in question.[1] Of course, in children's drawings and many other idioms of picturing, the form may be flat-looking, but if the drawing did not contain some perceptual cue that allowed the recognition of three-dimensional form, then we would not (without supplementary information) be able to tell if it were a picture of something or not.

All the existing philosophical literature, as far as I can tell, mistakenly assumes that planarity is tied specifically to perspective. As practicing artists know, however, it is actually intrinsic to picturing as such. Even an isolated, single three-dimensional item will, if it is foreshortened, have a frontal and a background plane defined by its nearest and furthest points in relation to the viewer. Planar structure, in other words, is not only an essential characteristic of the pictorial format as such but is repeated in the way the picture presents foreshortening and virtual recession. An artist can organize the main pictorial space of a work using further internal planes that parallel the frontal and background ones.[2]

In every picture there is a frontal plane that is notionally "closest" to an external spectator, that is, someone who sees the represented space as contained within the picture's physical edges. The frontal plane also defines the position of the notional internal viewer, that is, someone who might behold the represented scene immediately from within the picture.[3] This internal viewing position is vital, for even if there are features within the picture that seem to address an external viewer, such a viewer occupies a real time and space, which is different from that represented in the picture. This difference means that it makes no sense to ask, say, how far the external observer is from a church steeple represented on the picture's horizon but that it does make sense to ask such a question of the internal viewpoint insofar as it is a notional position within the same (pictorial) space as the steeple. It follows, therefore, that any element within the picture that appears to engage with an external spectator (e.g., in those cases where a figure in the picture seems to be looking at or even signaling to us) actually works by, in effect, having the external spectator identify with the notional internal viewpoint.

Such identification is fundamental. To see the picture in terms of its pictorial qualities (rather than as something just hanging on the wall) requires that we see "into" its pictorial space—we imagine ourselves being *in* there. By attending to this space and disregarding the real physical surroundings in which the identification takes place, the external observer identifies with what the notional internal viewer might "behold."

It should be emphasized, however, that this kind of disregarding does not entail the suspension of all beliefs and expectations bound up with the conditions of existence in real time and space. If it did, one would not be able to distinguish between the work's pictorial content and the contents of the real world. In fact, the wonder of picturing consists in its opening up a space that is both discontinuous with and different from the normal perceptual order while still being oriented by some of the demands made by that order, as well as by the external observer's own personal experience.

Now, the internal viewing position has a very distinctive character. In order to understand the ramifications of this, a contrast with photography is useful. The photographer takes the picture (or sets up the camera to take the picture) at a specific time and specific place; then the camera mechanically captures a momentary appearance of what is actually present before it. The relation between the photographic content and its internal viewer involves a *real* immobilization of *real* time, which means that the order of events from which the photographic image is captured is a spatio-temporal continuum whose existence as such is independent of the will of both the photographer and the spectator. The things in the photograph had a real history before the photograph was taken and went into a real future afterwards. One can imagine what this history or future might be like, but it existed or came to pass irrespective of our imagining; the internal viewer of the photograph witnesses an arrested reality.

Pictorial art is entirely different. It involves the *creation* of a virtual space that relates to the continuum of real space and time, but not in the way that the photograph does. When someone creates a picture, he or she creates a possible appearance of some three-dimensional item or state of affairs. Whereas what is photographed must have existed at some time or other, what is represented in a picture need not have.

The notion of possibility is important even for pictures that depict places, persons, or events that actually exist or once existed. We may know the picture's origins or iconography through collateral information, but so far as the pictorial format itself is concerned, we merely have the appearance of such-and-such a kind of three-dimensional form. It can be recognized in these terms whether or not there is collateral evidence allowing the subject matter to be identified. And even if we do have such evidence, there is no guarantee that the way in which the item has been represented is one that is true to some actual appearance or appearances of the object in question. Indeed, because the picture is an interpretation rather than a mechanical reproduction of its subject matter, variation from how such a thing appears or appeared in real life (in those cases where it did actually exist) will be built into the picture. It will always present a possible appearance.[4]

This is the key to picturing's metaphysical significance. Through being a *created* three-dimensional appearance the picture represents something that—in contrast to the photograph—does not have a past or future independent of the creator's or audience's will. The picture represents only a possible object of visual perception. Whereas the photograph causally arrests an appearance in the real spatio-temporal continuum, the picture's contents are virtual projections alone. True, the creation of the picture as a material thing involves its having a real past and (once created) a real future as a made thing. However, the virtual content of the picture as virtual exists at a different ontological level from this: it has been created through a medium such as drawing or painting.

Knowledge of this fact can, of course, lead us to treat the picture just as a physical object with a real past and future, but more significantly, it can lead us to recognize that the virtual reality that the picture represents is—by virtue of having been created—something apart from the temporal flow of the real world. This means that the picture's notional internal viewer and what that viewer beholds exist in a relation of idealized immobility (as opposed to the real, arrested immobility of the photograph), a relation I call "presentness."

The importance of presentness is as follows. Philosophers have often wondered at the nature of the "present" understood as an occurrent moment or instant in time.[5] However, the human experience of the present is more than just a temporal point or instant. It both connects and separates our experienced past and anticipated future. As a cognitive act or orientation, the present may last a mere instant or it may be more prolonged—as when we scrutinize something in perceptual terms. Whatever the case, the present has a profound significance in terms of human goals and fulfilment. We desire these to be realized in sustained terms, but such realizations mainly converge on the high points—on specific presents of achievement and gratification. While the present is thus a central focus of human existence, as soon as one reflects upon it, it has gone. Whether they are moments of achievement one has striven to attain or mere passing perceptual orientations, one present replaces another even in the very act of thinking about it.

The special importance of this is its regulative function in terms of the meaning of one's life. One strives for presents when everything falls into place or one attains the summits of fulfilment toward which one has worked. However, even when such privileged presents are enjoyed, we know that we are already passing on to something else—another goal or project in our life. We may find fulfilment in the culminating phases of a project or our life goals, but these do not crystallize in a single all-encompassing mega-present of achievement that endures through the passage of time. We may strive for its absolute possession, but to no avail—all we have are memories of it.

There is another aspect to the elusiveness of the present: its content is determined through the relation between that which is perceived and the character of the perceiver. In terms of the latter, how the human subject engages with the present involves different existential emphases—different styles of experiencing organized by the personal history that orients cognition and the social and cultural context of the agent's activity. However, these styles are of great psychological complexity. They draw upon many areas of memory and the habits and traits that define individual experience. One can reflect on these, but it is hard to comprehend their salient vectors in present experience itself. This is all to the good: if our sense of the present constantly reflected on the factors that enable it, then cognition would be overwhelmed by an excess of information that would leave it unable to make decisions.

It is these various aspects of elusiveness that the picture intervenes upon and transforms. To recognize the pictorial content as rendered in a medium is to perceive it as a possible visual present that is not embedded in or extracted from a real past or future. In this way, the notional internal viewer and what that viewer beholds are in a created and idealized relation of immobility. The transitory present is symbolically possessed and fixed in place. Indeed, through the artist's choice of materials and specific modes of handling, the personal existential style that informs any experiential present can be given a particular manifestation. It is made available to others as a possible way of seeing that the artist has completed.

Through this, the present's striving for self-possession, together with the style that both informs it and makes it meaningful, are objectively expressed in a reciprocal dependence. Presentness achieves, thereby, a complete idealization of the visual present. It allows both the transient present and the existential style that sustains it to be realized in a symbolically autonomous form. In this way, it is a metaphysical intervention on our experience of space and time.

All this having been said, two particular objections might be raised. First, it might appear that there is no conceptual basis for linking the notion of the present to picturing at all. It is true that some pictures involve reference to moments in time: if, for example, they depict movement or contain figures who appear to be looking directly at the viewer. But not all pictures are like this; a still life, for example, or a depiction of a rock or crystal simply presents one view of its subject matter. The possibility of a certain kind of spatial presence is depicted, but this need not involve any evocation of the present as a temporal concept whatsoever.

Against this objection it must be emphasized that three-dimensional spatial items—whether real or depicted—can only ever be perceived (at least by humans) under specific aspects, that is, as appearances of the item or states of affairs in question. And to appear under one aspect rather than another is precisely to be present to someone or something. The present in question can be a single moment or a sustained passage of time; but in either case, reference to a present of encountering is conceptually linked to the notion of something appearing.

Now, as we have seen, the picture depicts a possible appearance of some kind of three-dimensional item or state of affairs. Hence, even if a picture contains no overt markers, as it were, of the temporal present, it represents something that is made visible to both the internal and external viewer at some time or other; the present *must* be involved. It should be reiterated, however, that since, in pictorial art, this involvement takes the form of presentness, this feature's ideal immobility means that, in the picture, the distinction between objects in movement and those that are present statically to the viewer over a period of time is overcome. The experiential present is reconstructed in a virtual analogue whose essence is to endure even when depicting transitory events.

This leads to the second—and more substantial—potential objection. It might be claimed that far from being an idealized present, presentness is a kind of decapitation—an image that severs the present from the passage of time. Surely, however, *any* notion of the present (however one dresses it up) is only meaningful when fully connected to past and future—that is, as a feature within an integrated temporal horizon.

Now, it is true that in the foregoing account I have emphasized how presentness separates a notional present from the real order of past and future events. Nevertheless, this still involves reference to a horizon of time in notional terms. We will recall that the picture's viewer and the scene beheld by the viewer are related in an ideal immobility. This does not erase the temporal dimension as such—rather, it displaces it from the real to the level of possibility alone. Indeed, while what is "in" the picture does not have an actual past or future, we can at least imagine what a past or future for it might be like. And this is by no means an arbitrary act: the relation between the picture's virtual content and planarity can point in quite specific directions of notional movement through time—promptings that are of the greatest importance for presentness.

## II

As we have seen, the very fact that a pictured item or state of affairs appears as three-dimensional means that it is something that we know is not tied to just one appearance. Inasmuch as it is three-dimensional, it can, in principle, be seen from angles other than the one given and has other aspects that could be presented to the gaze. The possibility of change, movement, and thus of time is inscribed tacitly in the individual appearance, even if this does not correspond to some actual order of events in the real world. Moreover, as well as depicting individual objects, a picture can also present them in spatial relations with one another. In some cases this is simply because, say, the artist has done drawings of unrelated things on the same page of a sketchbook; one depiction may be above or below another one on the page, yet this may be simply a physical juxtaposition, not intended to depict some pictorial relation between the two items. It is only when a picture allows us to recognize that forms below and above one another on its physical surface can also be read as in front of and behind one another in virtual terms that we have our criterion of "pictorial space."

Pictorial space is of the most decisive importance for notional movement in the picture. Consider, for example, the small Burne-Jones picture *Study for Love Amongst the Ruins* (c. 1865–1870) (Figure 5). Here we have two different studies of the lovers rather than a single scene. The studies are separate, in that the upper image is not diminished or increased in size in relation to the lower figure. There is no perceptual cue that would entitle us to read it as being behind or above the lower group in a single scene; it is simply higher up on the sketchbook page, physically speaking. If one simply glances at this work, there may appear to be no significant recessional structure to it. However, as soon as one describes the planar structure of the individual studies, the recessional factor becomes manifest in each of them. In the lower study, there is a frontal plane that is defined by the passe-partout border (the "window" through which we look) and a central plane with its lower border defined by the feet of the female lover. The torso of the male figure is intersected by a plane of its own, although the figure's shoulders and left leg are breaking through it, obliquely. There is also a plane provided by the indeterminate background. The transition from foreground to central to background plane here describes the work's pictorial space. Any picture that involves presenting one thing as being in front of or behind another has something of the recessional structure described. As noted earlier, even children's pictures can be described in this way if they offer enough perceptual cues for us to distinguish relations of above and below from behind and in front of.

This example is just a simple illustration of pictorial space. It is through this concept that the relation between presentness and notional movement can best

FIGURE 5. Edward Coley Burne-Jones, *Study for Love Amongst the Ruins*, 1867–1870. Crowther-Oblak Collection, Ljubljana. Reprinted with permission.

be clarified. In the most general terms, pictorial space comprises three basic structural varieties.[6] First is an aggregate pictorial depth, where the apparent sizes of things change—albeit not in a calibrated way—on the basis of their distance from the viewer. This is the kind of pictorial space that was prevalent in the ancient world—the landscape motifs in the Pompeiian frescoes involve this mode of space—and it reappears in many modernist works, Fauvist landscapes being an especially good example.

The second major idiom of pictorial space is a planar unity, where the three-dimensional content is flattened out, appearing to be drawn toward the frontal plane; Byzantine and medieval religious art furnishes a good example of this.[7] Here a recessional element is present but is made entirely subordinate to the sacred narrative.

Pictorial space's third major structural idiom is one-point linear perspective, where objects diminish in exact proportion to one another the closer they are to a vanishing point situated on the horizon. This was first fully achieved in Renaissance Italy by artists such as Masaccio and Piero della Francesca. In it, the edge of the picture seems to define a kind of window through which a virtual spatial world is viewed.

Now, while each mode of pictorial space involves recession, the aggregate and linear perspective modes emphasize it. And once a pronouncedly recessional pictorial space has been created, then a notional relation to the future and the past is opened up within the internal virtual structure of the picture itself. Depth requires movement in order to be negotiated, and movement is conceptually tied to time—to moving into a future wherein our position in space has changed. Pictorial space suggests the possibility of such notional movement through its virtual recessional structure.

If it suggests this, then the possibility of such movement means that the presentness of the relation between the notional internal viewer and what such a viewer might behold is by no means a decapitation of the present. The notional possibility of alternative spatial viewing positions within the picture shows that the present relation between the internal viewer and the scene beheld is something that could be otherwise. A present relation can become a past relation insofar as the viewing position changes and "beholds" new appearances. The recessional structures of pictorial space locate presentness within a notional context of past and future. All aspects of the temporal horizon are internal to the picture, but in the form of represented possibility rather than ontological actuality.

The most dramatic exemplar of recession is linear perspective (though what I am about to say might be shown to apply to other kinds of perspective as well). There has been a great deal of rather misguided discussion of linear perspective, concerning whether it is privileged in terms of how we perceive things visually or just some culturally specific mode of representation with no special perceptual status.[8] This issue, however, is neither here nor there; linear perspective's real importance is its systematic visual presentation of possible positions in three-dimensional space from a two-dimensional planar base. If one wishes to exemplify the systematicity of a viewer's relation to the visual field within a two-dimensional medium, then perspective is the optimal means for achieving this. To explain: As a viewer moves through physical space, the appearance of surrounding things changes in exact and systematic correlation with the viewer's changes of position. There are constancies in terms of shape and color, but how they appear varies with our movements. Under ordinary circumstances, we are not explicitly aware of this systematicity; rather, knowledge of it functions intuitively so as to orient us.

Linear perspective is privileged in regard to this systematicity. It presents visual content organized in an exactly calibrated and gradual convergence upon a vanishing point placed at the horizon. This structure in itself suggests an unlimited and systematic continuation of visual space beyond the horizon and the side edges of the picture. The implication is that, for an internal viewer within the picture, his or her movements through perspectival space would give rise to corresponding exact variations in how things appeared to that viewer. The movements of both viewer and viewed would be correlated systematically ad infinitum, reconfiguring with each new position.

It is on these terms that linear perspective explicitly declares the systematicity of space. It involves a monocular planar immobilization of both the spatial items and relations involved and of the internal observer's view of them. Through this, the systematic character of these relations becomes a virtual alternative to the customary flow of visual perception. At the same time, however, it presents idealized vectors of notional movement wherein the viewer is linked not only to the immediately present scene but to possible changes of position that would be answered systematically by corresponding changes in how the surrounding visual field appeared. Space is disclosed as an infinite system of possible viewing positions each correlated exactly with the others.[9]

This means that the presentness or idealizing described earlier in relation to pictorial art extends not only to its representation of the present but also to the systematicity of space and movement expressed through it. Linear perspective declares presentness in self-contained terms and yet, at the same time, affirms its locatability within a notional infinite continuum of other such possible visual presents.

A vitally important qualification must now be made. Very few pictures have perspective worked out with insistent exactness. Unless a picture contains blatant perspectival inconsistencies, however, we will still tend to read it as if it were fully perspectival and thus subject to the points I have just made. Most pictures from the Renaissance onwards have this as-if perspectival character to some degree. It might even be described as the basic grammar of the Western pictorial tradition.[10] In the modern era, of course, many artists have broken with linear perspective, but even so, there are plenty of other modern artists in whose work the as-if perspectival orientation persists.

A case in point is Roger Fry's *View of Royat from the Parc Montjuizot* (1934) (Figure 6). Here the panoramic landscape does not emphasize linear perspective but nonetheless suggests it, through the finely calibrated harmonies of greens, grays, and browns that lead the gaze from the foreground into the virtual distance. The painterly and coloristic elements, in other words, are not features that overlay or conceal the work's perspectival "feel" but are actually responsible for it. If one looks hard enough in terms of technical scrutiny, perspectival inconsistencies or ambiguities may appear. But in aesthetic terms, we can simply enjoy the work's as-if perspectival idealization as it emerges from transitions of color and shape.

FIGURE 6. Roger Fry, *View of Royat from the Parc Montjuizot*, 1934. Crowther-Oblak Collection, Ljubljana. Reprinted with permission.

In the majority of modernist works (other than modes of expressionism, or loose impressionist idioms), in fact, an as-if perspectival orientation prevails. It is frequently less emphatic than in the Fry painting, but it is only challenged when, for example, things in the distance seem much bigger, perspectivally speaking, than those nearer the viewer. In such a situation, aggregate space displaces as-if perspective.

Thus, the metaphysical significance of presentness and the systematicity of pictorial space have been established. They are idealizations of our experience of the visual present and of the systematicity of its relation to space-time, the broader metaphysical and aesthetic implications of which can now be developed.

## III

Let us begin by considering the relation between spatiality and consciousness. The relation is complex, as shown by the following decisive passage from Gareth Evans:

> The capacity to think of oneself as located in space, and tracing a continuous path through it, is necessarily involved in the capacity to conceive the phenomena one encounters as independent of one's perception of them—to conceive the world as something one "comes across." It follows that the capacity for at least some primitive self-ascriptions—self-ascriptions of position, orientation, and change of position and orientation and hence the conception of oneself as one object amongst others, occupying one place amongst others, are interdependent with thought about the objective world itself.[11]

What Evans is pointing out is a conceptual truth about the reciprocal dependence of knowledge of objects and self-consciousness. This relationship centers on the subject's understanding of space-occupancy and the capacity of space-occupying things (insofar as they are enduring and reencounterable) to sustain such understanding. Movement through a systematic framework of stable space-occupying items and states of affairs is the basis of our capacity to be conscious of things and of the self. Human consciousness does not, in other words, gaze upon space from somewhere outside it; rather, the systematic character of space and its contents is what consciousness inheres in and where it finds its expression. The systematicity of space is both the body and dwelling-place of consciousness.

Pictures evoke this. They project places for exploration through virtual movement and perceptual relocation (as described in detail earlier). It

might be said, indeed, that pictorial space is itself an emblem of consciousness. Understood as systematically spatial, it is also an emblem of divine
consciousness—an exemplar of the sensuous divine, for reasons that will be
explained in detail below.

As a being with consciousness, God must perform specific acts of understanding. But these will have a comprehensiveness that is of an entirely different order from those of finite beings. God's thoughts will penetrate their object
and comprehend it exhaustively. They will be self-contained individual acts, yet
also ones that link systematically with all the others in a systematic, omniscient
consciousness. In God, individual acts of understanding and this omniscience
must, in a sense, exist within one another; they must have an absolute mutual
transparency, wherein the parts and the whole of consciousness inform one
another completely.

That this must be the case can be shown through a contrast with human
consciousness. For while such consciousness has present moments of specific
knowledge and awareness, these blur into one another in the flow of experience. Indeed, it may be that all such cognitive states are to some degree dependent for their individual character on their place in the developing whole of a
person's experience, but how they are shaped by the past or by anticipations of
the future we can never know conclusively. Finite self-consciousness is intrinsically opaque in terms of self-knowledge. It follows, therefore, that if divine
consciousness is to be different from the finite mode in a positive way, it must
be through the Godhead's cognitive acts being individually self-contained yet
absolutely transparent to one another—each thought intersecting with all the
others in an omniscient whole.

It is here that the arguments broached earlier concerning the metaphysics
of pictorial art come into play directly. We will recall that pictorial art embodies
presentness. The picture's notional internal viewer and scene beheld are joined
in a present whose immobility and self-containedness goes beyond what real
experience allows. Our human present and sense of the moment passes as soon
as it arrives; more generally, that which we seek in life tends to be something
that we are always on the way toward. Our moments of understanding and
achieved fulfilment are never fixed in place completely. This, indeed, is the very
essence of our finitude.

In presentness, however, a moment of appearance is made available as a
permanent possibility of experience. This self-contained character is matched
by the comprehensiveness of presentness. It makes its subject matter available

to the viewer in a cognitively more enhanced form than is allowed in ordinary vision. Specifically, it allows normally unnoticed details of how things occupy and appear in space to be made accessible to sustained perceptual exploration. In fact, if the work is genuinely artistic, we will return to it again and again, making new discoveries. It has a comprehensiveness that our ordinary perceptions of the present do not.

There is also a further advance on finite perception. For while the picture's virtual content has no real past or future, we can nevertheless (as noted earlier) imagine one for it; and even though we may not have created the picture ourselves, this imagined context allows us to make it uniquely ours. In real life, the story of one's past and how it led to the present, as well as the future that will come out from this present, both involve factors that are independent of our will. The past and future that we imagine for pictorial content, in contrast, are, by virtue of being imaginary, wholly subject to the will. We have notional possession of the present by virtue of controlling imaginary causal roads into and out of it; through presentness, our possession of the present is notionally completed.

It should be emphasized that all this happens through the picture's projection of a virtual domain of being that is manifestly other than the real finite order. Pictorial content presents a notional higher symbolic realm wherein the flow of appearances through time can be comprehended individually without being lost in the flux. From our external viewpoint, the presentness of the picture can be described as "eternalized."

Since, therefore, presentness exceeds the finite present in terms of its self-contained individuality, comprehensiveness, completeness, and overall eternalization, then there are grounds for claiming that it is sensuously divine through its symbolic affinity with God's individual acts of understanding in the sense just described. Indeed, through the making of pictorial art, we not only—as self-conscious and autonomous beings—exist in God's image but actually create ourselves in that image even more.

This first link to God's consciousness, however, can be understood in yet deeper terms. As we saw earlier, presentness encompasses spatial relations as well as immediately given appearance. Any recessional structure that positions one thing in relation to another in pictorial space creates thereby a notional context of past and future possible viewing positions. The represented present viewpoint is self-contained but can be recognized as one element in a system of other such possible viewpoints.

Linear perspective, or the as-if appearance of it, takes this to a higher level of completeness. It inscribes the present scene in a rigorous system of alternative viewpoints that unfold as the internal viewer explores the perspectivally rendered space. The rigor of the system is such that each potential viewing position within the system is equal to any other. Even though we may be presenting one scene in particular, it is, as it were, transparent to all the others as mutual elements within the systematic spatialization of the temporal horizon. In a curious sense each such possible element is omnipresent to all the rest. Here, in other words, at the level of space-occupancy we have an image that projects an ideal system of spatial knowledge whose linkage of the individual viewpoint in systematic reciprocity with the others can be interpreted as an image of God's own cognitive acts and their transparency to one another in his omniscience. It exemplifies the sensuous divine.

It might be objected that the real analogy that is pertinent here involves not the perspectival pictorial artwork but the relation between the systematicity of space itself and God's supposed omniscience. For the artist does not create spatial systematicity but merely translates it into a pictorial medium. If this is the case (the objection continues), then the proposed analogy is entirely unviable. The systematicity of space is no more than a system of formal laws concerning how items and states of affairs can occupy space and move in relation to one another, and upon which finite consciousness is dependent. Any analogy with divine omniscience is, at the very best, obscure and stipulative.

However, our experience of spatial systematicity in everyday life is mainly a practical thing without explicit vectors and structures except when thought about abstractly—in maps or geometry, for example. In such contexts there is no apparent link between spatial systematicity and the nature of consciousness. But when an artist creates a perspectivally ordered pictorial space (or what seems to be one), he or she opens (in ways described earlier) a privileged present viewpoint inscribed in a potentially infinite network of other, equal possible viewing positions. Here a perceptual viewpoint is linked to the systematicity of space in a way that allows us to think the connection through in deeper imaginative terms. On the one hand, perspective in pictorial art expresses that spatial systematicity which—as we saw earlier—is basic to consciousness as such; on the other hand, it does so in an idealized way that also sets it apart from space as immediately experienced through binocular vision.

If we think this expressive duality through in religious terms, the duality becomes a unity. We can regard artistic perspective as the sensuous image of divine omniscience because of its overtly idealized character—as a structure that represents the systematicity of space-occupancy—but at a metaphysical level of comprehensiveness and transparency (in the senses described earlier) that our experience of space does not attain. Our ordinary experience is inscribed within this ideal systematicity just as our spatially based finite self-consciousness inheres within God's omniscience. We cannot even begin to understand the absolute comprehensiveness and transparency of God's omniscience, but we can at least behold the sensuous image of it through perspective in pictorial art. To behold in these terms is, at the same time, to be joined with the Godhead, in symbolic terms.

For a secular thinker, all this talk of God and omniscience and so on will be scarcely credible. The religious interpretation just outlined, however, can easily be adapted to the secular viewpoint, because the experience of God in pictorial art is fundamentally aesthetic. Plane and perspective are metaphysical constructions but of a sui generis kind, insofar as they are distinctive to picturing as a medium. One can understand them in abstract terms (as here), but a full understanding only emerges when we engage with them specifically as pictorial—as features present to vision in the distinctive aesthetic unity of the pictorial artwork. It is this that makes them far more than metaphysical constructions per se. They involve, rather, metaphysical beauty. This means that our exploration of the formal and compositional qualities of the work are taken to another level by reference to the implications of presentness and those of perspective, with its "as-if" forms.

Through metaphysical beauty we gratify our longing both to enjoy the fruits of a finite world and, at the same time, to suspend the conditions of that finitude through the attainment of something more enduring. This is an intense psychological completeness. Pictures project the possibility of the divine sensuously, through structures that symbolize it; they are aesthetic intimations of Godhood. For the secular thinker, the experience of such imaginary Godhood is a release from perceptual limitations as such—a fantasy of becoming God-like. For the believer, the picture's Godhood is something to be lived in—as a transcendence of the finite self toward a living God. How one inhabits Godhood is a matter of faith, but the inhabiting of it completes the self, and more.

## IV

Metaphysical beauty in the sense just described can answer another profound question. The question concerns why pictorial art is of such transhistorical and transcultural significance—why human beings find it so recurrently fascinating. Scientific and anthropological approaches would probably answer that there is nothing more to this than the simple fact that picturing as a visual phenomenon is especially effective in making facts vivid to the senses; it has informational potency. But an answer of this sort is reductive, to say the least. Pictures can indeed convey visual information, but this does not in and of itself rule out the intrinsically fulfilling metaphysical beauty just described. Indeed, the very emergence of the concept "art" as a set of practices that are meaningful over and above their informational and practical functions suggests that the relevant media—including picturing—must have some kind of intrinsic fascination.

So again we must ask how this is possible. The obvious response is to link pictorial art to aesthetic experience, usually understood in terms of expressive qualities. But this again leads to a question, namely: "Why is pictorial art the kind of thing that people can find expressive—what is special about it?" One answer might be that it is expressive in the way the other art forms are—through having some enhanced unity in terms of the cohesion of formal and (where relevant) narrative elements. However, while this may be true, it is also clear that such cohesion is embodied differently for the different media involved: literature and music are organized around the unified linking of events in time, whereas the cohesion of picturing centers on the unity of the spatial object. Literature and music achieve expression in one way and the pictorial arts achieve it in another; it is this distinctiveness of expression that has to be explained.

In the case of pictorial art, some explanations have been offered. The most sustained approach is that of Richard Wollheim, who identifies a phenomenon—"twofoldness"—that is distinctive to the making of pictures. It centers on our capacity to see three-dimensional things "in" the picture's surface. While seeing the surface and seeing the thing in it are logically distinguishable, they are perceptually inseparable. As Wollheim puts it: "They are two aspects of a single experience, they are not two experiences. They are neither two separate simultaneous experiences, which I somehow hold in the mind at once, nor two separate alternating experiences, between which I oscillate."[12] When it comes to explaining what gives pictures their expressive qualities, Wollheim emphasizes only that the artist's thoughts, beliefs, and emotions find expression when the artist creates twofoldness. At no point, however, does he explain what it is about twofoldness itself that allows the artist to make any kind of existential investment—expressive or otherwise—in it. Why should it matter to us at all?

Formalist approaches have also had difficulties with the expressiveness of pictorial art. Clive Bell, Roger Fry, and Clement Greenberg, for example, have tried in their different ways to identify features distinctive to art's mode of aesthetic experience, but as I have shown elsewhere,[13] these are highly problematic, offering no adequate explanation of what makes "significant form" significant. The nearest we get to this is Bell's neglected discussion of the "Metaphysical Hypothesis." He asserts that what we respond to when we enjoy "significant form" is an emotion experienced by the artist, which is "transmitted" to us, and through which the real significance of form is elucidated. According to Bell:

> Instead of recognizing its accidental and conditioned importance, we become aware of its essential reality, of the God in everything, of the universal in the particular, of the all-pervading rhythm. Call it by what name you will, the thing that I am talking about is that which lies behind the appearance of all things— that which gives to all things their individual significance, the thing in itself, the ultimate reality.[14]

At least Bell goes beyond Wollheim insofar as he explains *why* a factor distinctive to the visual arts—namely, forms based on harmonies of line and color— might be found expressive. But he does not explain how these formal features are able to engage with those metaphysical concepts on which he grounds form's ultimate expressive power. In what sense is God in everything? And if God is like this, what idiom of consciousness is involved?

So this is the problem. Existing approaches simply do not explain what it is about pictorial art that makes it expressive. And when religious explanations are invoked, they are often too general to be of much use. The way in which something is done—in this case the artist's style—can, under normal circumstances at least, only matter to us if what the style presents—in this case the phenomenon of picturing—is also of importance to us. What has to be explained, in other words, is how artistic style engages with humanly important factors that are basic to the ontology of the medium; only in this way will pictorial art's distinctive mode of intrinsic aesthetic fascination be explained.

The discussions of ideal beauty in previous chapters have offered some elucidation of this intrinsic fascination. The present chapter offers another, through the metaphysical significance of pictorial presentness and its idealizations of our space-time experiences. Through these features, pictorial art intervenes upon and transforms how visual reality appears. If the artist makes a picture that draws attention to how it has been created, it can invite us to imagine ourselves as symbolically joined to God's omniscience or to fantasize about occupying the spatial world in a God-like way. Either interpretation involves metaphysical beauty based on factors distinctive to pictorial art. Such transcendence explains a key aspect of why this art medium has enduring expressive significance. Metaphysical beauty offers a level of symbolic completeness in terms of how we belong to the universe as a whole. We have the feeling of being far more than merely physical creatures.

That being said, it should be emphasized that many other factors in addition to the metaphysics of plane and perspective contribute to pictorial art's intrinsic fascination. But given metaphysical beauty's grounding in the (at least) imagined metaphysical victory of infinite consciousness over finite limitations, it has a prima facie entitlement to be regarded as one of the most important of these factors. It helps explain why art really matters to us, why it is a psychologically completing activity.

The pictorial phenomena of presentness and the all-important perspectival and as-if perspectival variants of pictorial space are metaphysical reconstructions that idealize experiential time and space. They are the basis of a distinctive pictorial metaphysical beauty. The link between spatiality and consciousness allows us to interpret pictorial space—especially in its perspectival or as-if perspectival modes—as emblems of divine consciousness and the inherence of spatially based finite consciousness within it. This metaphysical beauty may be interpreted in religious or secular terms and helps explain the intrinsic aesthetic fascination of pictorial art.

## Conclusion

It might be thought that what I have been describing is a highly complex set of phenomena that has little relation to our ordinary aesthetic experience of pictures. However, it can equally well be claimed that presentness and the imaginative occupancy of an idealized space are actually very common experiences indeed. If something is pictured, then we know that its appearance will be fixed in that form for as long as the picture exists. We experience presentness in a crude, even nostalgic way. And even though we usually negotiate pictures in terms of the visual narratives or information that they present, there are other, wistful moments when we imagine what it would be like to enter the scene represented.

There are many occasions in life—especially aesthetic ones—when one has basic experiences such as these but feels that there is so much more to be said about them—if only one had the words. I have tried to provide a few words of the relevant kind—to show some of the deeper factors that might be involved in the simple aesthetic responses just described. I have provided reasons why we are entitled to link pictorial cognition to metaphysical beauty.

For the secular thinker this beauty involves the sensuous divine and nothing more. It terminates in an exhilarating exceeding of finite barriers that is, in the final analysis, no more than a loss of self based on an aesthetically pleasing illusion. For the religious believer, in contrast, pictorial cognition offers an image of the divine derived from an ontological realm—the spatial and corporeal— that at first sight seems very alien to the notion of an infinite spirit. Metaphysical beauty involves an imaginative bonding with God's being that is richer than that achieved through understanding alone. Indeed, to fully comprehend what it means to be created in God's image requires that our experience embrace the existential fullness of this creation, in terms of sensibility and affect, hopes, felt limits, and aspirations as well as mere thought. The metaphysical beauty of pictorial cognition exemplifies this fullness: the viewer both feels and exceeds his or her finitude through participating in an image of God's total possession of the present and/or divine omniscience.

There is one important qualification, however. While planarity and perspective are fundamental to pictorial cognition, they are not the basis of any hierarchical distinctions in the pictorial arts. All pictures have planar structure; what is decisive in aesthetically energizing it as a metaphysical construction is how the individual picture articulates its specific three-dimensional content in a plane. Similar considerations hold in terms of perspective as well. Indeed, many works using aggregate or planar unity to organize their pictorial space are far superior, artistically speaking, to many perspectival works. And if a work does have perspective, the decisive factor in the aesthetic energization of its metaphysical significance is *how* it is represented. Without distinctiveness in this respect, the metaphysical beauty will be lost among the picture's broader visual functions.

# 3 TRANSCENDENT SUBJECTIVITY

## *Kant and the Pictorial Sublime*

## Introduction

The aesthetic transcendence involved in the sublime, the subject of this chapter, can be explained by critically reworking Kant's theory of the sublime.[1] The most important source for this theory is his *Critique of the Power of Judgment*.[2] Before addressing Kant's theory, however, one of its limitations must be noted at the very outset. For him, the sublime arises specifically from the experience of nature; he refuses to accept that it can also be experienced through artworks. Nevertheless, and of course inconsistently, he sometimes uses examples of artworks or cognate artifacts in the course of illustrating his theory.

Kant's insistence on this disqualification of art from the sublime has been received very sympathetically in some quarters, notably by Emily Brady, one of the most important recent supporters of Kant's theory of the sublime, who argues that

> insofar as some artworks attempt to catch the sublime, they fail to have the impact of natural sublime experiences, with the multi-sensory and forceful character of first-hand engagement with storms, raging seas and so on. Although the arts may seek to depict, express, embody, or in other ways convey sublimity, the particular combinations of qualities and effects characteristic of this kind of aesthetic response cannot really be captured. In essence, art fails to deliver the whole package.[3]

For Brady, the factors that comprise this "package" include scale, formlessness, wildness and disorder, and emotions and imagination. The claim is that since the sublime centers on these, then the artwork—confined as it is as a product of artifice—cannot deliver the experience. In effect, Brady is restricting the authentic experience of the sublime to nature.

This stipulative procedure, however, does not work. First, given wild nature in all the terms described, it is interesting that some people are simply not impressed. "You can stuff all this, I'd rather be at home by the fire." The problem here is that whether or not one is susceptible to the features described by Brady is surely contingent upon individual taste and sensitivity. It may be that a person does not care at all for the sublime in outdoor nature yet adores representations of it. It is entirely possible, in fact, that there are people who are so profoundly sensitive to such representations that their feelings and imaginations become wholly engrossed by the artistic presentation. The images in storybooks or pictorial novels, for example, may have this effect; many people, indeed, can have experiences such as these with images in art galleries. All that is needed is for the artwork to operate with the same perceptual cues as found in the natural sublime and to instantiate these in a distinctive way.

Second, it should be emphasized that the very attempt to restrict the sublime to the natural variety is counterproductive with respect to the Kantian sublime itself. The great importance of Kant's approach is that it identifies a basic cognitive structure—the interaction of perceptual and imaginative limitation and rational comprehension—that can, irrespective of Kant's narrow understanding of it, be embodied in different contexts and by different objects. The sublime is not some exclusively natural experience but a family of experiences that cluster around the basic structure. In previous chapters we saw how ideal beauty in classic art has its origins in an existentially broader notion of ideal beauty. The same holds for the sublime: the pictorial sublime is a more particular expression of the metaphysically profound structure first identified by Kant in relation to nature, but it possesses much broader application.

I

To understand Kant's theory requires, first, a clarification of some of his most basic philosophical concepts, notably, "understanding," "imagination," and "ideas of reason." Understanding involves the application of concepts; it is the basic recognitional activity wherein we judge that $x$ is $B$ or whatever. According to Kant, imagination allows what is not present (e.g., things from the past, future possibilities, or possible states of affairs as such) to be mentally represented in quasi-sensory images. Through this, the understanding can engage with items, times, and places other than those presently given. In effect, imagination provides the conditions that enable concepts to be formed and applied.[4]

The rational idea has a more ambiguous role. For Kant it is the idea of a maximum or complete state of something that is never actually attained in experience. The idea of infinity is an example of this. However, Kant also seems to identify it with a general striving for completeness in our comprehension of phenomena. He says, for example, that the "voice of reason . . . requires totality for all given magnitudes, even for those that can never be entirely apprehended although they are (in the sensible presentation) judged as entirely given, [and] hence comprehension in one intuition."[5] Reason, in other words, sets standards of comprehension for our experience of phenomena. It challenges sensibility and imagination to match its standards of completeness. This means not merely apprehending a phenomenon as something there but registering it through a single perception or image that comprehends the complexity of its total appearance part by part.

This is where the experience of the sublime begins. For Kant, the sublime is an aesthetic judgment with a distinctive form involving a "mental movement" from an initial feeling of pain or privation to one of pleasure. It has two varieties, the mathematical and the dynamical, which we shall now consider.

Mathematical sublimity arises when rational beings encounter some perceptually overwhelming item or set of items. Suppose, for example, that we perceive a vast phenomenon. If it is beheld at a distance, we can easily recognize that it is a vast phenomenon with some of its aspects hidden to us, but which aspects those are we could imagine, if called upon, from our present perceptual viewpoint. Here, in Kantian terms, we simply *understand* the phenomenon's vastness.

On some occasions, however, even things beheld at a distance are found sublime. In such cases we do not merely recognize the phenomenon as being vast; rather, its vastness provokes reason's demand for completeness of presentation. In turn, this challenges the imagination to form a presentation that comprehends all the units or elements from which the phenomenon's vastness is constituted. But imagination is overwhelmed by this task.

Before we discuss this in more detail, we need to address another problem. Kant provides plenty of examples of phenomena that are experienced in terms

of the sublime, but he is not precise about what it is about them that leads reason to place such a demand on the imagination in the first place. This is a significant weakness, for clearly not every vast phenomenon is experienced as the
sublime. Therefore, we need to explain why the vastness of some phenomena
provokes reason and overwhelms the imagination, while the vastness of others
is simply recognized as such, and no more than that.

A useful guide is provided by Kant's claim that phenomena that occasion
the sublime are "counterpurposive." In layperson's terms this means that there is
something about the phenomenon's sensible structure that overrides our normal
tendency to simply recognize it as a vast example of a thing defined by such-
and-such a group of properties. Though Kant himself would not allow it, we
could quite reasonably add that specific perceptual cues provided by vast phenomena could be the factor that awakens reason's demand for the comprehension of totality. The possession of such perceptual cues is what sets the sublime
object apart from those that just happen to be exceedingly large, or whatever.

Kant's basic approach, then, can be developed through the description of
relevant kinds of perceptual cues whereby vast phenomena are recognized and
that also stimulate us to comprehend their phenomenal totality in imaginative
terms. These cues include the following:

(1) *Insistent repetition.* This occurs when an item's component elements or a
series of items present visual rhythms that seem to suggest indefinite continuation beyond the limits of the perceptual field. Here, our sense of what
the thing is, is overwhelmed by the challenge to form an image or images of
the parts or forms that suggest such indefinite continuation.

(2) *Insistent and/or complex irregularity or asymmetry, or exaggeratedly large
size.* Here a familiar kind of vast thing is configured or encountered in a
context that deviates from the customary appearance of things of this kind
and thus challenges us to consider how this deviation is possible through
attentiveness to the many parts that it involves. But precisely because it is a
deviation (is, in some sense, "monstrous"), the usual "formula" of the whole
does not apply, and thus the parts seem to be set loose into formless diversi-
fication. We cannot form a stable image of the vast whole because the principle of its unity has broken down; there is the suggestion of sensory chaos.

(3) *Animation or the suggestion of it.* Very large phenomenal items or states
of affairs are usually stationary. When set in motion—as in the case of a
stormy sea or a windswept forest—the motion of the individual elements,
their overlaps, and their potential for further motion attract our perceptual

attention. Even static phenomena such as mountains and mountain ranges may set up visual rhythms that challenge us to imaginatively comprehend all the elements that compose the (apparently) animated body.

(4) *Suggestive concealment.* If a large thing is concealed by mist or shadow, this can provoke us to imagine all the parts that are thus hidden. The more visually interesting the idiom of concealment, the more keenly will our imagination try to comprehend the vastness that is so concealed.

These perceptual cues, then, explain why some vast phenomena challenge us to comprehend their phenomenal totality, in a way that others do not. When it comes to describing how such phenomena engage reason and imagination, however, Kant offers a convoluted and confused account of what this involves.[6] According to him, when a phenomenon's vastness attracts our attention, we seek to find an appropriate measure whereby its size can be made comprehensible. This involves an "aesthetic estimate," that is, a measure based on something sensibly given.

Curiously, however, Kant holds that in the case of vast phenomena, the only appropriate measure is infinity itself. While infinity is intelligible as an idea, however, it cannot be adequately realized as an aesthetic estimate: it cannot be comprehended adequately in a single perception or image. In trying to assimilate the parts of the phenomenon in a single image, the more of them we apprehend accumulatively the more we lose track of the parts registered earlier in the process. The attempt to frame infinity as a measure breaks down—the imagination is overwhelmed.[7]

Kant's strained attempts to assign a role to infinity is one of the major reasons why his account of the sublime is so difficult. Ironically enough, there is no philosophical necessity to invoke it at all. The very fact that we are led to search out an absolute measure for the vast phenomenon in the first place logically entails that its vastness has already been found overwhelming. It is blatantly obvious that we are dealing with a phenomenon whose many parts or aspects are not going to be comprehended by the imagination in terms of a single image. The process of seeking out infinity that Kant describes, in other words, is superfluous; imagination is overwhelmed without our ever having to bring in infinity as an aesthetic estimate.

That being said, there are some occasions when the infinite may indeed play a role. The perceptual cues described earlier may involve parts or hidden aspects of the vast phenomenon that appear to be continuable beyond the immediate perceptual field. In some cases, this suggestion of continuity may take the form of an apparently endless continuation toward infinity. Thus a role can be found for infinity, even though one need not bring the idea of the infinite into every experience of the sublime. Nevertheless, this role is of some interest, and we will return to it later.

The task before us now, however, is to explain how, for Kant, the feeling of privation arising from the overwhelming of imagination gives rise to a feeling of pleasure. Again, his own account is extremely confused, conflating two basic but different explanations of the positive aspect of the sublime. He himself emphasizes an explanation with moral implications whose significance we will consider later. The first (and much more economical) approach is embedded in Kant's theory but not spelled out in explicit terms. It is simply as follows. Reason's demand for imagination to comprehend the vast phenomenon in a single presentation is a demand that cannot be met. But the very fact that imagination is overwhelmed makes the extraordinary scope of human reason vivid to the senses. We cannot imagine the phenomenal totality of the vast phenomenon in a single presentation, but we can nonetheless comprehend it as a rational idea. All phenomena—no matter how colossal or vast—are finite. Reason tells us that they form limited wholes no matter what their magnitude.

This rational capacity, however, is something that we mainly take for granted and use without remarking on it. If we do regard it more reflectively, it is usually in the course of thinking about such things as problems in philosophy or science or the implications of technology, or as a result of religious questioning. When vast phenomena provoke reason in the way described, however, then imagination's failure to meet the demand means that the transcendent scope of reason is made vivid at the level of the senses.

One can think about the scope of reason by means of reason, but in the present case it is made into something aesthetically pleasurable through being manifested at the level of the senses itself. In this way, our existence as beings who are both rational and sensible is brought into a harmonious reciprocity. While imagination is overwhelmed, this overwhelming acts as a springboard for reason to come alive at the level of perception itself. The sublime is a distinctive mode of aesthetic judgment.

Though this account offers a sufficient explanation of our pleasure in the mathematical sublime, Kant offers a second approach to the problem. As we have seen, he claims that, faced with an overwhelmingly vast phenomenon, we try to imaginatively comprehend its vastness by searching out an absolute "measure" for it, namely, infinity itself. We have seen that there is no need to introduce infinity as a necessary feature of the mathematical sublime, as Kant does, but that one can find a place for the suggestion of it—through the perceptual cues whereby vast phenomena make us attend to their vastness.

That Kant wants infinity to play a necessary role is very instructive. For him, reason involves not only understanding and agency but also our capacity to act in accordance with principles, be they theoretical or practical. Moral principles are the most complete expressions of reason, because they are unconditionally binding upon us by virtue of being rational. They are also the purest expression of freedom, because acting upon them involves reason alone and excludes our animal desires or impulses. Reason elevates us above nature.

This is the basis of Kant's second explanation of the positive aspect of the mathematical sublime. He tells us that "the feeling of the sublime is . . . a feeling of displeasure from the inadequacy of the imagination in the aesthetic estimation of magnitude for the estimation by means of reason, and a pleasure that is thereby aroused at the same time from the correspondence of this very judgement of the inadequacy of the greatest sensible faculty in comparison with ideas of reason, insofar as striving for them is nevertheless a law for us."[8] In these remarks, Kant appears to think that he is explaining why we find the mathematical sublime pleasurable; but he is actually doing no such thing. As we have already seen, our pleasure in the mathematical sublime centers on imagination's being overwhelmed in a way that affirms the superiority of rational comprehension. But in the foregoing remarks Kant says that the pleasure arises because this superiority is judged by us to be in accord with what is "a law for us," namely, realizing the demands of reason in the face of natural challenges.

Here, in other words, Kant is not actually offering another explanation of why we take pleasure in the mathematical sublime. He is, rather, confusing its aesthetic grounds with elucidation of the broader, moral implications of the experience. Fortunately, this elucidation has its own importance. Our capacity to experience things aesthetically—and especially in terms of the sublime—discloses broader truths about the human condition and its place in the cosmos. In this respect, Pascal famously observes: "Man is only a reed, the weakest thing in nature, but he is a thinking reed. . . . If the universe were to crush him, man would be nobler than his destroyer, because he knows that he dies, and also the advantage that the universe has over him; but the universe knows nothing of this."[9]

Pascal's observation can be integrated with Kant's elucidation of the mathematical sublime. While human beings are less than miniscule specks in the immensity of the physical universe, they are nonetheless specks with the capacity to comprehend the idea of the beginning and end of all things, the size of galaxies, and the idea of infinity itself. Reason is not only a basis of subjectivity, it is the dimension wherein the subject transcends its physical limitation in the most extraordinary way. It comprehends things that utterly exceed the limits of what we can perceive and imagine.

The decisive point is that while these insights can be framed as ideas, in the sublime it is nature itself—both as phenomena and in terms of our natural perceptual and imaginative being—that in effect emphasizes our special place in the universe. No matter how imaginatively overwhelming phenomena may be, we thinking reeds are able to comprehend them. Here, the truth of our being-in-the-cosmos is felt as well as thought; we comprehend in the fullest terms.

Kant's mistaken explanation of the grounds of the mathematical sublime thus invites us to elucidate its significance in these directions. We might not agree with his rigid interpretation of what reason involves, but it is most certainly reason's directing of our animal nature that is distinctive for how we inhabit the world. It is not the whole story, but it is the basis of our vocation. The experience of the mathematical sublime discloses this vocation.

## II

Let us turn now to Kant's account of the dynamical sublime. His approach to this is rather different from his approach to the mathematical mode. For a start, whereas the mathematical sublime pertains to vastness, the dynamical mode is about powerful phenomena, considered under the specific aspect of their capacity to destroy us. According to Kant, if such a phenomenon is beheld from a position of safety, we recognize that it could destroy us, but this provokes thoughts concerning the fact that we are much more than merely physical beings, subject to the mechanistic workings of nature.

> It calls forth our power (which is not part of nature) to regard those things about which we are concerned (goods, health and life) as trivial, and hence to regard its power . . . as not the sort of dominion over ourselves and our authority to which we would have to bow if it came down to our highest principles and their affirmation or abandonment. Thus nature is here called sublime merely because it raises the imagination to the point of presenting those cases in which the mind can make palpable to itself the sublimity of its own vocation even over nature.[10]

In other words, fearful objects provoke our awareness that while nature can destroy our physical body, it cannot destroy our rational, spiritual being. Humankind's rational self-awareness is special, because—at the very least—human beings are free to make choices on the basis of principles rather than through mere responses to stimuli alone. The most distinctive aspect of our human being, in other words, is "supersensible" (Kant's term). We are sensuously affected creatures, but insofar as we can act through principles as free agents, we must assume that the most decisive aspect of the self is seated beyond the mechanistic operations of the natural world.

For Kant, the supersensible self and its principles of agency are constitutive of our human vocation. In the humdrum of everyday life and its decisions, however, the structure and scope of this vocation are easily lost sight of. The dynamical sublime counters this: perceiving a fearful phenomenon from a position of safety can make the meaning and scope of freedom vivid precisely through our thinking of it in this sensuously intense context.

Now, before addressing specific problems in Kant's account, we must ask the same question that arose in relation to the mathematical sublime: Why is it that only a few fearful phenomena are found sublime? What separates them from run-of-the-mill fearful things encountered from a position of safety? The answer is, surely, perceptual cues of the kind already described in relation to the mathematical sublime. In fact, the very same cues are involved: insistent repetition of parts, insistent irregularity or asymmetry of parts, exaggerated size, animation, and (especially) suggestive concealment all emphasize the threatening aspects of phenomena. As features of a dynamic phenomenon or force, they suggest a general dissolution into parts, fracturing and breakage, the destructive energy of animated powers, the hyperpower of the gargantuan, the suggested horrors of the unknown. Recognized on the basis of such cues, in other words, the fearful aspects of phenomena are especially emphasized at the perceptual level; it is this that allows them to be a source of the sublime.

All this being said, Kant's account of the positive factor in the dynamical sublime—awareness of our supersensible vocation—does not dwell easily with the sublime's aesthetic character. It appears to be a moral and metaphysical insight that arises when we perceive certain kinds of fearful phenomena. In some people, an encounter with fearful phenomena may involve imaginings of moral defiance of the kind described by Kant, but many cases—erupting volcanoes, tidal waves, haunted-looking houses, and the like—can surely be found sublime without the involvement of any of the moral conjectures described by

Kant. Indeed, there is no immediately apparent reason why these moral conjectures should be the ground of a specifically aesthetic pleasure.

Fortunately, there is again a much more economical way of articulating the dynamical sublime that avoids the difficulties that arise from Kant's special interests. Instead of emphasizing the fearful character of the phenomenon, we can emphasize instead its destructive power or its suggestiveness of such a character (Kant's own examples, indeed, are very much in this vein). We know, of course, that the phenomenon has immense destructive power of a sort that we could not hope to comprehend in a single "presentation"—it simply overwhelms the imagination. But as in the case of the mathematical sublime, we can nevertheless grasp its total destructive capacity as a rational idea. What could wipe us out physically in an instant can be comprehended through reason; in this respect, our rational power exceeds that of the phenomenon.

On these terms, then, the dynamical sublime should be regarded as structurally akin to the mathematical mode. In the latter, the limits of imagination in the comprehension of vastness make the scope of reason vivid to the senses; in the former, imagination's inability to adequately comprehend destructive power makes us all the more aware of our extraordinary power of reason.

Thus, it can be claimed that Kant's own explanation of our pleasure in the dynamical sublime, while confused, has a broader elucidatory potential, just as we saw with his account of our pleasure in the mathematical sublime. In this regard, it will be recalled that Kant takes the pleasure to arise from conjectured moral defiance when beholding fearful phenomena from a position of safety. While these conjectures do not, for reasons noted earlier, actually explain the grounds of our pleasure, they are instructive. For example, if one believes that the self has a supersensible basis in the soul, then one might be inclined to elucidate the pleasure we take in the experience of the dynamical sublime in further directions. One would not just experience the destructive power of the phenomenon as comprehended by and affirming reason; one might also think of the test of faith—of belief in the soul—that might be required if the phenomenon were actually threatening. In this case, one might say that the appearance of destructiveness makes vivid—in sensible/imaginative terms—what faith might demand of the believer under circumstances of mortal danger. This is not sufficient for a global explanation of our pleasure in the sublime, but it could be the basis for a specifically religious version of the dynamical sublime.

The elucidatory potential of Kant's mistaken explanation can be taken further to encompass a related special case, an iconographical version of the dynamical sublime. As an example, we might consider martyrdom—a religious phenomenon, mainly, but also a historical one, as many people have given their lives for political cause and country and the like. Let us consider Tintoretto's *The Crucifixion* (1563–1566). The Crucifixion has been represented many times by many different artists—so much so that it risks being something of a cliché; Tintoretto's treatment, however, is one of those that break through convention.

The work is on a vast scale (201 × 482 in. [518 cm × 1,224 cm]). Christ gazes down from the cross so as to comprehend the mass of humanity disposing itself beneath him. His friends and family are overwhelmed by grief, while the other groups of figures go about the ordinary labors involved in erecting the two other crosses. The groups depicted have different vectors of activity, whose conjunction creates an overall sense of restlessness. Life must go on for whatever purpose; in the bustle and energy of this scene there is a brutal indifference to the meaning of what is being done specifically. This indifference is accentuated by the arched back of the donkey (center left) and some of the incidental detail in the mourning group (bottom center left), which suggest the sinister empty eye socket and gaping mouth of a skull. It is in this context of grief and indifference and the presence of death that Christ must countenance his redemptive role and interrogate the grounds of his own belief in it.

A very different work is James Tissot's uncanny *View from the Cross* (1886–1894), a picture that is only 9 × 10 in. (25 x 23 cm) (Figure 7). Here the usual viewing conventions concerning the Crucifixion are transformed: we see the scene from Christ's subjective visual viewpoint. This reversal is all the more unsettling because Christ's redemptive role as a personal savior involves our having a personal relationship with him. Here we are summoned to understand his suffering and what is at stake in it. Through being shown his viewpoint we are invited to comprehend his martyrdom in a way that we did not expect; the limits and fraying of corporeality are framed within the scene that we behold through Christ. In this respect, the distribution of white and related colors across the onlookers—and the vertiginous height from which we view them—makes it seem as if individual figures are gradually becoming insubstantial and tending toward spectral forms.

In these two artworks, a scene of fear and suffering is transcended. Through the artists' presentation of the New Testament narrative, we comprehend the nobility of Christ's resolve and are invited to identify with it. These are not, of course, cases of the viewer countenancing fearful natural phenomena, and therefore Kant himself would not have regarded them as dynamically sublime.

FIGURE 7. James Tissot, *What Our Lord Saw from the Cross* (*Ce que voyait Notre-Seigneur sur la Croix*), 1886–1894. Brooklyn Museum, New York, N.Y. Purchased by public subscription.

But the same dynamics are at work: the fearfulness of a situation and a remarkable individual's negotiation of it challenge us to share the same moral resolve. Here, the natural limits of the human body and its capacity for suffering tell us that there is a hope of salvation, if only we have the faith and/or the moral courage to embrace it.

There is another key difference between this approach and Kant's own position. A positive response to the threatening events represented (and in the case of the Tissot picture, even to recognize what is going on) logically presupposes that we know the iconography of the work—the specific narrative that is being depicted. This means we must recognize the figure of Christ and what his passion signifies. In Kant's theory, direct perception of a real danger (albeit from a position of safety) is what occasions the dynamical sublime. But here we find it arising through recognition of a particular narrative representation, together with its implications. There need be no real danger present at all. Such an iconographical version of the dynamical sublime can, of course, extend beyond religious art; in the final part of this chapter I shall consider an important contemporary example of it that involves the greatest moral profundity.[11]

If Kant's own explanation of our pleasure in the dynamical sublime does not work in relation to purely natural phenomena, it nevertheless directs us toward a specific body of artworks that may be regarded as dynamically sublime in some respects, inasmuch as—if we understand their iconography—they generate an appropriate spiritual message from a sensible/imaginative presentation of destructive events.

Let us turn to the psychological character of sublime experiences—the profound sense of transcendence that characterizes them. While we cannot imaginatively comprehend the phenomenon's vastness or power/fearfulness, we are, in effect, symbolically transported by the affirmation of reason that this gives rise to. In some people, this may involve a feeling that he or she has literally transcended the limitations of the body. The vast and/or mighty phenomenon unfolds in all its imaginatively overwhelming immensity, but once the totality of this has been comprehended as a rational idea, then the vastness and/or power of the phenomenon is no longer a frustration. We can almost, so to speak, "surf" its accumulating revelations of parts or the fearful power evoked because they have been contained by rational comprehension.

In other people, the experience involved may be more intuitive. There is no need to engage in any imaginative apprehension of the phenomenon's parts or power in an occurrent way because the perceptual cues whereby it engages our interest already tell us that this will be futile. Yet as soon as we recognize the phenomenon in these terms, we know equally intuitively that no matter how big or powerful it is, it has a limit; the phenomenon's imaginatively overwhelming character tacitly underlines how far reason's power of comprehension can take us.

We have seen, then, that Kant's basic approach to the mathematical and dynamical sublime can be adapted to yield a highly unified theory. Both varieties of the sublime involve a mode of affective privation that gives rise to a pleasure in the scope of reason. We may sometimes think that vast or powerful objects are overwhelming, and we may sometimes realize the extraordinary scope of human reason. But in the experience of the sublime these two aspects form a whole that is more than the sum of its cognitive parts. Each aspect engages with the other, so that perceptual/imaginative response and rational insight are wedded to one another—the sublime is a distinctive aesthetic experience.

We have also seen that while Kant is especially prone to error in explaining our pleasure in the sublime, the explanations he offers have a high level of elucidatory interest in regard to the moral and religious implications of the sublime; and we have considered some highly interesting iconographical examples. This raises the key question of how the Kantian theory should be more specifically contextualized in terms of pictorial art.

### III

First, it is important to emphasize the following point. In Kant's own accounts of the mathematical and the dynamical sublime, he makes much of the involvement of imagination as an occurrent factor. In perceiving the vast or powerful object, the imagination huffs and puffs trying unsuccessfully to digest, as it were, the overwhelming "input." A skeptic might simply deny this outright, saying, "I find the Alps sublime whenever I see them, but I don't engage in the struggle to imagine that you describe."

Against the skeptic, however, there are aesthetic experiences where our sense of finitude does play an important mediating role. The question is, how? Interestingly, the answer lies with perceptual "cues" as triggers of the sublime. We recognize what these cues tell us: that what is given here, if we attended to it long enough, is a phenomenon whose size or power would quickly exceed what we can imagine. This means that the overwhelming of the imagination need not involve some occurrent struggle; rather, it is simply an anticipated outcome that we can "read off" from our recognition of the appropriate cues.

This is especially important for pictorial art (a point that adds further to the refutation of Emily Brady's position at the beginning of this chapter). In this regard, it is interesting that even the largest frescoes or paintings on canvas are very rarely, if ever, of a size that is genuinely perceptually overwhelming in terms of vastness or power. Nevertheless, the character of what is represented and how it is represented in terms of such features has a key and felicitous significance, owing to the fact that pictures are spatial items that open up a virtual three-dimensional space by means of artifice.

In nature itself, the occurrence of sublime-evoking perceptual cues depends on how the relevant objects happen to be configured; it is down to luck and chance. In pictorial art, in contrast, the artist projects a scene using virtual cues of this sort created as compositional factors in the particular work. If it is done formulaically, of course, the work will be a "sublime-type" picture and will not engage our imagination. But if it is artistically insightful in terms of style, it will engage us and perhaps even astonish us through the way in which such phenomenal vastness and/or power has been understood and projected by the artist. Even though the represented phenomenon is overwhelmingly vast or mighty, the artist has created perceptual cues that evoke this. Here, the evocation of vastness or might makes the power of artistic vision vivid to the senses.

Of course, other media such as literature and music can address overwhelming phenomena in ways that make the scope of literary or musical composition vivid to us. But they are not spatial. The picture is tied to a delimited portion of space, which means that for it to really engage our imagination through its projection of a vast three-dimensional phenomenon, it must be of the utmost visual felicity. The limits of the picture's edge and the physicality of the painted or drawn surface (as well as its relative flimsiness) are restrictions that the pictorial evocation of virtual vastness or power has to overcome, in a way that other media do not. The overwhelming projection has, as it were, to burst from a manifestly confining momentary glimpse of spatial expanse (i.e., the "presentness" described in the previous chapter). This does not make it superior to the other media; indeed, literature and music doubtless have their own special features with respect to the sublime. But it is, nonetheless, a difference that gives a distinctive character to how pictorial art evokes the mathematical sublime.

Consider, for example, John Martin's mezzotint *The Evening of the Deluge* (1828) (Figure 8). This work is a key pictorial expression of the sublime in its representation of the greatest extremes of nature in vastness and power, about to wash away physically insignificant human forms. But the destructiveness of this is contained by the fact that Martin has articulated it in visual terms. He has turned the imaginatively overwhelming into an affirmation of the scope of artistic creativity in finding a way of articulating this overwhelming scenario in a single visual moment.

This can be done in less dramatic ways as well. Consider, for example, Alfred William Hunt's *A Stream in a Moorland Landscape* (c. 1870) (Figure 9). This image is watercolor with scratching-out and is a mere 10 × 14 in. (26 × 36 cm).

FIGURE 8. John Martin, *The Evening of the Deluge*, 1834. Mezzotint.

FIGURE 9. Alfred William Hunt, *A Stream in a Moorland landscape*, c. 1870. Crowther-Oblak Collection, Ljubljana. Reprinted with permission.

Hunt suggests mist swathing the tops of the hills and an emphatic panoramic distance between the foreground and background. However, the ruggedness of his technique creates a pitted surface that influences how we perceive not only the land but even the sky, investing the work with a sense of pervasive desolation broken only by the strategic placing of two unidentifiable objects in the lower left–center distance. Yet even these markers of distance, as it were, have no recognizable character beyond the fact that they are upright, which adds to the overall eeriness of the scene. Hunt's picture is not, of course, a major work, but when viewed directly (rather than in reproduction) its imaginative evocation of raw natural vastness makes the scope of artistic creativity vivid in a more subtle way than does the Martin work.

How, then, does the pictorial sublime compare with other representational visual media such as sculpture and photography? In regard to sculpture, there is a qualitative difference from picturing insofar as, by definition, sculpture must incorporate some real three-dimensional spatial material. Suppose a free-standing sculpture is extraordinarily large, like the Colossus of Rhodes; this might link it to the sublime, but it would be through the immense physicality of the work making the scope of sculptural vision vivid to us. Indeed, the use of real three-dimensional material as such means that sculpture evokes the sublime differently than pictorial art. The appearance of physical and spiritual motion in a work such as Bernini's *Ecstasy of St. Teresa* is amplified by the fact that we know the representation to be done in marble. The very contradiction between the inert, cold reality of the stone and the ecstatic animation of its sculpted configuration makes the extraordinary scope of sculpture vivid.

Matters are different again in the case of photography. For example, many of Ansel Adams' works are panoramic landscapes that evoke a sense of magnificent spatial recess beyond the horizon. They instantiate the spectacular sublime through the way the photographer's angle on this scene has selected features that imaginatively activate our sense of it "extending beyond." But our perception of this is informed by knowledge of photography's causal rigidity (discussed in the previous chapter). Here, the evocation of the sublime has a poignancy not found in other art forms, precisely because it is the causal imprint of a vastness that really is or was.

In all these cases we can have the sublime; but the differences among pictures, sculptures, and photographs mean that the evocation of vastness has a different aesthetic emphasis in each. Ontological differences give the sublime corresponding variations of aesthetic effect. We have the same experience, structurally speaking: a represented excess that makes the scope of artistic creation vivid at the level of space-occupancy. But this gives rise to different avenues of correlated existential associations by virtue of medium-specific features.

Interesting effects can also be achieved through combining different media. Indeed, in the postmodern era there has been a great willingness to explore in these directions, often with special attention to the negative factor in the sublime that arises from overwhelming complexity or horror.[12] The work of the contemporary Israeli artist Bracha Lichtenberg Ettinger provides a case in point. Theodor Adorno famously remarked that after Auschwitz there can be no more lyric poetry.[13] This may, in fact, be the opposite of the truth; after Auschwitz there *must* be lyric poetry. The question is, what form should it take, given the catastrophe in question? Ettinger's works that combine paintings and photocopies explore this without declaring themselves to be visually lyrical. That quality emerges (in a qualified way) only through a process of suffering and empathy achieved through her creative process—a process centering on a mode of creative remembrance that offers an element of symbolic redemption for what was lost in the Holocaust.

In Ettinger's major works of the 1990s, this involves a literal deconstruction of pictorial media as well as the expectations that are specific to them. Consider, for example, *Autistwork n. 1* (1992–1993) and *Eurydice n. 23* (from a series done between 1994 and 1998) (Figures 10 and 11). Both works appear to be based on the same infamous grainy photograph of Jewish women (including one with an infant in her arms) awaiting their horrifying fate. To understand what is at issue in such works, we must first consider some remarks concerning the nature of photography.

Photography as a medium is based on a causally rigid relation to that which it is a picture of. Given a genuine photograph, we know that its subject matter once existed. The image used by Ettinger evokes all too well Roland Barthes' ideas of the intrinsic relation between photography and mortality: the women in the picture are dead, and yet they are going to die. The image is testimony to the fact that the women are dead, but it also serves to render some moments before their death permanently captive. How may one release them from captivity?

In *Autistwork n. 1*, Ettinger sets up a photocopy of the infamous image. As a copy of a photograph, this in itself puts one more remove between the spectator and the women represented. But then Ettinger intervenes upon this distance: she interrupts the photocopying process so that it is not carried through into a visually precise image. This yields an unfixed residue of powdered ink

FIGURE 10. Bracha Lichtenberg Ettinger, *Autistwork n. 1* (1992–1993). Photo courtesy of the artist.

FIGURE 11. Bracha Lichtenberg Ettinger, *Eurydice n. 23* (1994–1998). Israel Museum Collection, Jerusalem. Photo courtesy of the artist.

that the artist then colors with pen or brush. Specifically, the gaps between the particles of ink dust are filled so as to form a kind of aesthetic membrane that both clothes the image and offers a gesture of respect and healing toward the women. This membrane also engages the viewer through the unexpected transformation that it works upon the image. Griselda Pollock notes that Ettinger's technique here is based on "patiently painting the place where the grains of ink were deposited on their journey towards the image and thus towards the traces of the people once photographed and inadvertently memorialized."[14]

It is important to emphasize that what is involved here is not only a deconstruction of the fixity of the photographic image and its relation to memory—an opening up of the vastness of human relations and histories embedded therein—but also a questioning of the character and scope of beauty when faced with subject matter that involves evil beyond all comprehension. In this respect, Ettinger's personal investment in the colors she works with is relevant. As she has said, "White, black, and violet are already almost too much. White I tell myself could tell about black and more. Violet cuts through them like a wound, or like a scar, depending on the moment."[15] *Eurydice n. 23* is based mainly on two of the colors that Ettinger mentions. Her use of violet invests the image with a ghostly and nightmare quality, which is amplified by the sinister black forms (suggesting camp buildings and smoke) that loom above an extended horizon stretching more or less from one edge of the picture to the other. The violet membrane clothes the figures, but a nightmare quality arises from the way it seems at the same time to be a stretching and smearing of the women's skin.

The courage of Ettinger's vision is manifested in precisely this effect. It is through her colors that she clothes and respects the women, and by altering their tragic final appearance she invites us to regard them in terms of a subjectivity that transcends catastrophe. But at the same time, how can such a gesture begin—in even the slightest symbolic terms—to offer any redemption? This is why the visual transformation achieved in Ettinger's picture might be read as acknowledging its limitations, through being at the same time the very factor that emphasizes the nightmare quality of those captured and horrendous moments from the past.

All these points converge on a feature that the artist may not even be aware of. It is a very simple thing: when tears fall on a photocopy, they disturb its fixity and may result in transformations similar to those worked by Ettinger. Perhaps this is the real unconscious of her work. Through exploring her own creative artistic individuality, she has found a way to make the photographic image symbolically weep for its own content, and through this, to allow inhabitants of the present to honor the worth of those who were lost. While this is a simple fact, it has real redemptive depth. As the rabbi at the funeral of the Jewish children murdered in Toulouse in 2012 said, "We weep because we are strong."

This is how lyrical art can survive after Auschwitz. Its lyricism must be a yea-saying to life that emerges through wrestling with evil. It must be the positive element of the sublime, where the artist's power of empathic intervention is made vivid. Ettinger's art faces evil and attempts to deal with it through deconstructing existing categories of representation, namely, photography, photocopying, and painting, for ends that involve an overlapping—perhaps even integration—of the moral, the political, and the aesthetic.

It is this that completes the link to the sublime. Earlier we saw how Kant's explanation of our pleasure in the dynamical sublime is unsatisfactory but has elucidatory potential. One aspect of this is its directing us to an iconographical version of the dynamical sublime, where recognition of its fearful character (e.g., the Crucifixion) involves understanding its narrative context. Ettinger's work is like this. At first glance it has the appearance of a melancholy lyricism, but once we understand the nature of her photographic sources, the fearful character of what is presented in the work becomes manifest. And when we understand the implications of her creative process, this offers a moral position wherein even incomprehensible evil cannot triumph. Such evil is acknowledged and at the same time overcome through the very means whereby it is acknowledged, namely, artistic creativity.

In these terms, Ettinger's work is an important evocation of the ethical limits to the sublime. Scenes of vastness and destruction make the scope of human reason and art vivid to the senses, but this transcendent subjectivity can be abused—when reason and art are appropriated for oppressive ends. Reason and art are always haunted by the ghost of a possible regression to animality, as embodied in Nazism and its *Kultur*. Ghosts are elusive things that can be negotiated through forgetting or being ignored; but in Ettinger's pictures, the ghost is trapped and made to answer.

## Conclusion

In this chapter we have seen how Kant's argument that the experience of the sublime involves an interaction between constants in human experience—namely, the limited scope of perceptual and imaginative comprehension and the comprehensive power of reason—can be reconstructed. The sublime, in both its modes, aesthetically exemplifies how cognition can exceed the limitations of finitude. This is embodied by pictorial art in its own distinctive way, in both the pictorial representation of overwhelming spaces and fearful phenomena and, more subtly, when knowledge of a picture's iconography allows it to evoke extremes of experience.

# 4 COLOR-FIELD ABSTRACTION
## AND THE MYSTICAL SUBLIME

## Introduction

Mark Rothko has been quoted as saying that "a painting doesn't need anybody to explain what it's about. If it's any good, it speaks for itself."[1] But how is it possible for a painting to "speak for itself" when it does not represent recognizable kinds of three-dimensional items and/or states of affairs? If Rothko's claim is to have any truth, it must be based on some dimension of intersubjectively intelligible meaning in abstract works. There is a theory that explains how this intersubjective intelligibility is possible; indeed, it allows us to identify notions that enable abstract works to "speak for themselves" in even more specific terms.[2] This theory shows abstract art to be an *allusive* mode of picturing.

## I

Let us begin the elucidation of the theory of meaning for abstract art with the following observations. Abstraction emerged under specific historical conditions in which artists were exploring the boundaries of figurative meaning, hoping to go beyond them. This "going beyond," however, still has one feature in common with figurative idioms, namely, the presumption that the painted or sculpted work is about something other than its status as a mere physical artifact. In other words, it refers to something over and above the mere reality of its existence as a material thing. Of course, in some minimalist works the affirmation of this may be exactly what the work is "about"; but if this is the case, then it is representing its status as a material thing, rather than simply being one. Indeed, when an abstract work is presented as art in a presentational context, none of its immediately visible properties are virtually inert or neutral. No matter how mundane it may appear at first sight, it has been positioned in terms of potential virtual content.

The question then arises as to what this content might involve; and the answer is optical illusion and/or visual aspectuality. In regard to the former, as soon as one places a mark or line on a plane surface, it can be seen as situated upon or incised into that surface. It will open a relation of figure and ground, where the mark will function as a figure that is in front of the ground or as a ground that allows a larger surrounding figure-space to show through in front (in effect, the mark appears to puncture the picture plane). It will also have a further optical character determined by its relation to the edge of the surface.

Even minimalist works involve the presumption of virtuality. In Robert Morris' *Slab* (1966), for example, the mass and volume of the painted stainless-steel rectangular prism suggest heaviness and intense quiddity, but the lack of emphasis on surface texture and detail can also make the work appear insubstantial. An imaginative dialectic of being and nonbeing is provoked by the work's being visible under both these aspects. The relation between the two accordingly gives the work a virtual meaning over and above the mere fact of its physicality.

If optical illusion / aspectuality is the basis of reference in abstract art, a further—and decisive—question arises as to what it refers to. Abstractionists often suggest "spiritual reality," but they interpret this in highly specific ways that would involve knowledge of the artist's own theory in order for the nature of its application to the artwork to be understood. However, it is notable that abstract works find appreciable audiences even among observers who know nothing of the artists' theories; they find the work meaningful within the work's own internal resources.

How is this possible? It might be suggested that forms in abstract art are found formally and/or expressively significant in aesthetic terms. But if it is the former that is the case, we must explain why form can be found intrinsically pleasurable and what separates this from mere pleasure in ornament or decoration; if the latter is the case, we must explain on what grounds the work is expressive and how its expressiveness compares and contrasts with bodily expression. At some point, in other words, we must insist on criteria of formal and expressive satisfaction.

Fortunately, such criteria are available. For if we find abstract forms intrinsically meaningful, this must be through some reference to features that are basic to how vision and the body inhere in the world. Figurative art refers (virtually) to the realm of recognizable three-dimensional items and states of affairs and their spatial interrelations; it creates a visual illusion of what it represents. Abstract works, in contrast, allude to the "transperceptual space" of hidden or unnoticed visual details, textures, and relations, as well as alternative possible perceptual or imaginative viewpoints on them, that are the "stuff" from which the world of recognizable visual three-dimensional objects is emergent. Such features are as much an aspect of the visually real as are the things we see directly. They traverse perception (even if not explicitly noticed), and in other cases they may become visible if our bodily orientation changes, or if we supplement our present visual perception by imagining the hidden aspects of things or how they might appear under different perceptual circumstances.

Transperceptual space is clearly of great complexity. It may nevertheless be analyzed in a rough-and-ready way in terms of the following aspects:[3]

(1) Imagined presentations of spatial items, relations, or states of affairs that are not accessible to perception under normal circumstances, are incompletely available, or are so taken for granted as usually not to be noticed. These include such things as forms on the margin of the immediate visual field, microscopic structures or life-forms, the visualization of internal states of a body or state of affairs (e.g., seen in cross section), and unusual perceptual perspectives (such as aerial ones). This aspect also includes real or imagined features or details of specific visual appearances separated from the whole of which they are a part.

(2) Possible visual items, relations, states of affairs, or life-forms as they might appear in perceptual or physical environments radically different from the usual. This might be applied to ordinary environments that have undergone radical visual transformation (e.g., through the intrusion of evanescent atmospheric effects or physical catastrophe, or as experienced in dreams); subterranean, subaquatic, and possible extraterrestrial environments; and effects arising from inhibiting or distorting the normal conditions of visual perception.

(3) Visual forms that appear to be variations upon recognizable kinds of things and/or their relations and spatial contexts without amounting to actual representations of them. This can involve apparent distortion or fragmentation of a thing or state of affairs, or perhaps partially remembered details of things we have experienced that suggest them without presenting enough familiar aspects to allow them to be conclusively identified.

(4) Idealized variations on features basic to the structure of visual perception, including mass, volume, density, shape, positional relations (such as "in front of" or "behind"), and color. In some abstract works, these features are presented (individually or in concert) as purified foci of attention in their own right rather than factors embedded in the everyday visual world of things and artifacts.

(5) Visual correlates of states of mind. Specific kinds of shapes and colors—and the relations between them, of course—carry strong emotional connotations. These are partly a function of natural factors, but more pervasively, a shared cultural stock of such connotations. Suppose we find a shape threatening. It may seem that we cannot explain why it is threatening, but with more sustained reflection we recognize that its threatening character arises through suggesting something like an arm caught in the act of delivering a violent blow.

I am proposing, then, that transperceptual space consists of at least five aspects based on visual detail, possibility, or association, all of them involved (usually without being noticed) in our visual recognition of things and states of affairs. Which of the aspects is to the fore in a particular abstract work is determined by the visual character of the work itself; in many cases, more than one aspect will be involved.

It might be objected that all this reduces the representational content of abstract art to what the spectator can "read into" it. But this is not the arbitrary factor it might seem to be. If, for example, I point out that Jackson Pollock's *Full Fathom Five* (1947) suggests patterns of subaquatic or extraterrestrial vegetal formations, I can justify this interpretation by identifying specific features and relations in the painting. The fact that these involve seeing the work's content under different aspects is not an inconsistency. Abstract works do not represent specific, recognizable kinds of three-dimensional objects (except occasionally as an element situated in a broader abstract content); rather, they *allude* to possible transperceptual visual items or states or affairs. They are, in effect, pictures that allow us to negotiate the aesthetic potential of that which, for various reasons, is marginal in our normal visual perception of the world.

There are, of course, limits to this. If, for example, I saw the Pollock painting as a herd of gazelles seen from an aerial viewpoint as they stream majestically across the veldt, or if I were to insist that the painting alluded to a cross section of an avocado pear, then it would be much harder to make such virtual meanings stick; they would not—in terms of their virtual visual properties—be consistent with being perceived under such aspects. The criteria for relating abstract works to transperceptual space, in other words, are flexible but not arbitrary.

To sum up: The virtual three-dimensional reality opened up by the optical illusion and planarity of pictorial space in abstract art should be taken to be that of transperceptual space. Our perception of abstract art is informed, intuitively, by reference to this. The configuration is intelligible through its consistency with some possible transperceptual state of affairs. It is pictorial through allusion rather than direct depiction—though occasionally abstract works incorporate depictive elements, set loose from their usual referential moorings.

## II

The ways in which abstract artworks allude are a function of individual tendencies and styles. Let us focus on a particular one, which relates to a mystical version of the sublime that has not been discussed before. Understanding it involves reference to three metaphysical factors. First, as we saw in the Introduction, the notion of something's existing is not intelligible without reference to space-occupancy: to exist means to occupy space or to be an effect of relations between space-occupying bodies and/or forces.

The second metaphysical factor is linked to the first. Space-occupancy involves finite items, states, and events together with relations between them—that is, elements that come into being and then pass away. Let us call this "becoming." A rational animal can comprehend the idea of becoming as such, but he or she cannot perceive it at the sensory level in this "pure" manner; rather, we experience it as exemplified in different kinds of phenomena and relations between them.

The third metaphysical factor is an ultimate question, with two overlapping and probably inseparable aspects. Why does the universe exist, and why does it exist in the way that it does? Science can identify ever more comprehensive causal relationships and structures among elements of matter and the character of space-time. At best, however, these are descriptions based on relations between quanta; they may explain *how* things come to be, but not *why* they come to be.

There are, of course, many possible answers to this, but there are at least three core positions available. First, we might settle for the idea that reality is not the kind of thing that can have a reason for its existence. This can be one of the most profoundly disturbing thoughts of all: in a universe without a reason for being, everything that comes to be must pass away absolutely into nothingness, the void, lingering only in memory until the memory bearers themselves pass away. But there can also be a positive obverse to this, for precisely because all things pass away without any enduring remainder, it becomes incumbent upon us to value what exists, while it exists, all the more intensely—cherishing the beauty of passing moments and configurations. A reality without reason has the capacity to both terrify us and enhance our valuation of it in equal measure.

Now, this existential understanding of reality is by no means the only one with a dual emotional aspect. There is an interesting second position that involves the most extreme variety of philosophical monism. Suppose, as in early Hinduism and some strains of Western absolute idealism, it is claimed that the idea of the universe being sufficiently composed from individual items and relations is demonstrably self-contradictory. The phenomenal world is the mere appearance of an ultimate reality or absolute that reaches beyond the limitations of space-time and gives the universe a reason for being. The absolute comprehends itself through the finite spirits that are integral aspects of its own identity. We are not chance aspects of this reality; rather, through our self-consciousness its own identity is completed. We struggle to formulate the truth and scope of this mutual dependence, but as finite beings can only comprehend it in a partial way. Our attempts are beset by contradiction as soon as they address the big cosmological questions. (There are, for example, equally good reasons for believing that the universe had a definite beginning in space-time and for arguing that it cannot have.) Despite this frustration, however, we are driven not only to give voice to our inherence in the absolute but to clarify this inherence in a way that satisfies both reason and our felt need to belong.

There is, finally, a third and much more familiar way of answering the ultimate metaphysical question, namely, through belief in a personal creator, God. God is of such incomprehensible power and majesty that the very concept of the divine being is overwhelming—even terrifying—in its scope. We feel inadequate to and unworthy of even the task of understanding. Yet the universe was created for creatures to inhabit and recognize the signs of God's love and presence. Finding our personal way to the creator brings fulfilment through the diversity of ways in which this love and presence can be identified and responded to.

The existential, monistic, and theistic ways of answering the ultimate metaphysical question, then, each have a dual structure, that of the emotionally negative compensated for by positive understanding and feeling. If we are honest with ourselves, however, it is very likely that as fallible creatures we are often caught between elements from all three answers, and perhaps others besides. Rational consideration of them takes us just so far, and it is here that the possibility of getting it all wrong becomes most nagging. There is some act of faith involved in accepting any answer to the ultimate metaphysical question; when we flip from one possible answer to another, the issue of faith becomes a source of acute uncertainty and anxiety. Indeed, even for those of settled theistic faith, a certainty of belief cannot (without a colossal arrogance at odds with our finite rationality) transform the incomprehensibility of the divine into a simple set of signs that the faithful need only decode.

To understand how these considerations are basic to the mystical sublime, we must now consider the mystical and the sublime in turn. There are at least two major criteria of the mystical. First, such things as nature (be it in general or in its individual manifestations), existential predicaments, and artworks often seem to have a superabundance of meaning that seems familiar and/or "right" yet that we cannot sufficiently paraphrase in ordinary language. They show or suggest meaning, rather than speak it directly; meaning emerges as something hidden between the lines of normal, discursive strategies of reason.

Now, if mystical insight is a special mode of understanding, then it will surely involve indirect meaning along the lines just described. Such indirect meaning, however, is also a feature of how artworks engage us aesthetically per se and of uncanny experiences and coincidences in general. Hence, in order to be distinguished from these, mystical insight should be identified only with those cases where indirect meaning points toward the ultimate metaphysical question and possible answers to it. In turn, mystical insights concerning these questions and answers become sublime when they evoke all the frustrations described earlier, in a way that vivifies both the scope and the limitations of our rational comprehension of the ultimate.

This, of course, is a special case of the structure that Kant identifies, which we considered at length in the previous chapter. The mathematical and the dynamical sublime involve an excess of phenomenal size or power that makes the scope of rational comprehension vivid to the senses. Mystical sublimity, in contrast, is a more unsettling experience in relation to both aspects of the basic excess/comprehension structure because it arises from something that is felt to be without reason, or is experienced as radically unknowable in phenomenal terms, or involves both these things. We can comprehend something of all this, but only incompletely. The positive element in the mystical sublime, in other words, is ambiguous, insofar as the shadow of the inexplicable or unknowable is felt even within our powers of rational comprehension. We can comprehend or articulate the overwhelming feature, but only in terms whose limitations are also acknowledged. Problems of doubt can emerge. Accordingly, the mystical sublime is more existentially complex than other modes of sublimity.

A key transition can now be made. In Section I it was posited that aspect (4) of transperceptual space includes idealized phenomena and relations that are presented in a purer visual form than that in which they usually exist. It can be shown that there is a mode of abstract art that idealizes the very relation between becoming, space-occupancy, and the mystical sublime, through an emphasis on fields of form and/or color. This art is a variety of what is usually known as color-field abstraction, which has been associated historically with Barnett Newman, Mark Rothko, and Clyfford Still. It is the first two of these artists who can be linked to the mystical sublime;[4] we shall deal with them in turn.

## III

In 1948, Newman created *Onement 1*. In this small work—27¼ × 16¼ in. (69.2 × 41.2 cm)—a dark, brownish-red background is divided directly in the middle by a vertical band, composed from masking tape left in place and painted over with a lighter cadmium red. The band both connects and divides the elements in the field. This vertical "zip" (as Newman described it subsequently) hereafter became a key compositional factor in animating his fields of color.

A simple structure of this kind is often associated with geometrical abstraction. But Newman's treatment of it lacks the clean finish that often characterizes geometric works. There is a suggestion of something hidden, or isolated, or even lost or broken. At the same time, a fundamental optical ambiguity is created: the zip seems to sit upon the void and appears to be before it (in every sense), but the zip can also be seen as a small vertical gap through which a mysterious light is shining. This very ambiguity means that a relation between an individual and a surrounding space is declared wherein the individual can be regarded as both enclosed by the space and as the means whereby an alternative space shows through. There is here a profound and irresolvable dialectic between material reality, with its inescapable finitude, and spiritual reality, as a mode of illumination and comprehension.

This aesthetic symbolism explains why Newman himself regarded *Onement 1* as so important. Even before it, he was using titles that describe or connote ultimate states of being or relate individual persons to such states. Through all this,

Newman was literally trying to give art a new meaning after the Holocaust by finding a mode of visual expression that evokes the existentially and metaphysically ultimate. *Onement 1* constitutes the breakthrough, but one other major transformation gives Newman's work its distinctive character, namely, the sheer size of his subsequent paintings: *Vir Heroicus Sublimis* (1950–1951), for example, is 7 ft 11⅜ in. × 17 ft 9¼ in. (242.2 × 541.7 cm). Even if Newman did not always work on this scale, scale becomes an important factor in his work. In effect, Newman realized the importance of space-occupancy—in terms of both the physicality of the painting and of the artist—as a basis for the aesthetic expression of metaphysical meaning. Indeed, in conversation with Thomas Hess in 1966 he insisted: "What I'm saying is that my painting is physical and what I'm saying also is that my painting is metaphysical. What I'm also saying is that my life is physical and that my life is also metaphysical."[5]

To make more sense of these remarks, let us focus on the series of fourteen works in relation to which they were made, namely, *The Stations of the Cross* (begun in 1958 and exhibited in 1966; the whole series is in the National Gallery of Art, Washington, D.C.). Each is around 78 × 60 in. (198 × 153 cm), which means that they are far bigger than the average human yet still on a human scale in terms of the physical encounter with them. This in itself is of importance because in engaging with the works there is a sense of our normal human condition being pulled or extended in both physical and spiritual terms.

The subject matter of the work alludes, of course, to Christ's Passion and Crucifixion. Newman's interest, however, was not in the episodic narrative details of this but rather Jesus' cry to God: "Why have you forsaken me?" This (in its Aramaic original, "lema sabachthani") in fact featured in the actual title of the exhibition. In the interview with Hess, Newman explained that he had always wondered why—after forgiving those who had persecuted him and were in the process of executing him—Jesus should ask such a question of his Father.[6]

So how should we characterize Newman's paintings in terms of such meaning? A useful starting point is the medium itself. The most striking feature of the works is that major areas in most of them are left unpainted to reveal a raw, white-colored canvas. His color range throughout the series is extremely limited, consisting only of the raw canvas and some white magna, together with black magna used mainly in its own right though also occasionally laid on thin or smeared to produce gray effects.

The basic compositional structures are minimal, restricted to blank fields of raw canvas, or in a couple of cases black and in one case white fields. The zips and their various articulations are rendered in black or white verticals of varying thickness. In the *First Station* (Figure 12), a black zip some two or three inches thick adjoins the left vertical edge of the picture. A much thinner vertical white zip divides the canvas about two-thirds across. Black and gray smudged forms attempt to wrap themselves around this vertical, through uneven visual oscillations distributed from top to bottom; in some areas they corrode the zip's edge boundaries, but at no point do they cover it completely.

The *Second, Third,* and *Fourth Station* continue this basic spatial format, each having a left-edge vertical zip and then further zip activity about two-thirds across to the right. Newman diversifies the zip structure in each of the pictures. The oscillating blacks and grays appear again in the *Third Station* but this time in a significantly diminished form (Figure 13). It is clear that the spatial format common to these works affected him powerfully, for it was while working on the *Fourth Station* that he found the idea of a series expressing "lema sabachthani." He kept to the raw canvas and limited color range, as this would allow him to "maintain this cry in all its intensity and in every manner of its starkness."[7]

In the remaining works, a key transposition occurs in the *Ninth Station,* when Newman renders both the broad left-edge zip and those that are two-thirds across in white paint on the raw canvas ground (Figure 14). The *Tenth Station* produces a disturbing variation on this (Figure 15). It alludes to one of the earlier works, namely, the *Fifth Station,* where the broad left-edge black zip is rendered "pure," as it were, but with the appearance of destabilization (with the beginnings of a splatter effect) down the full extent of its right-hand side. In the *Tenth Station,* a thin, white zip (adjoining a broad left-edge one) appears to be caught in a more advanced stage of decomposition, with its dissolving splatters suggesting an ultimate decay. The suggestion of this, however, is played off against a very broad (stabilizing) white zip that encompasses the entire right edge of the painting. The stabilizing factor is also central to the *Fourteenth Station,* which completes the series; Newman paints the entire field in white, with a gray zip at the right edge of the canvas.

This brief formal analysis provides a way of answering why Newman's basic spatial format and explorations of it should illuminate Christ's "lema sabachthani" question. It is noteworthy that Newman titles the works with numbers only and that he only arrived at the subject matter of the series while working on the *Fourth Station.* We must read them not as episodes in the culminating narrative of Christ's earthly existence but as states of mind that individually

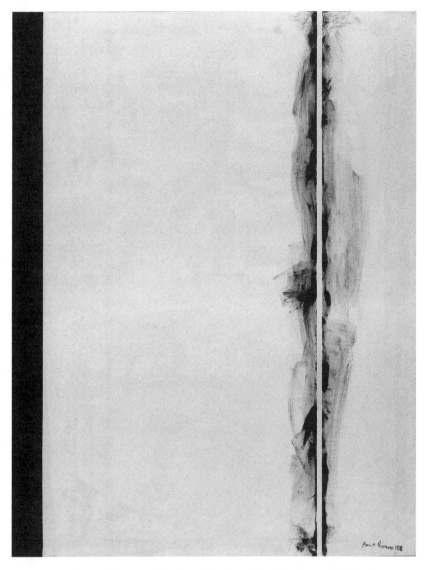

FIGURE 12. Barnett Newman, *Stations of the Cross: First Station*, 1958. © The Barnett Newman Foundation, Artists Rights Society (ARS), New York / IVARO, Dublin (2015).

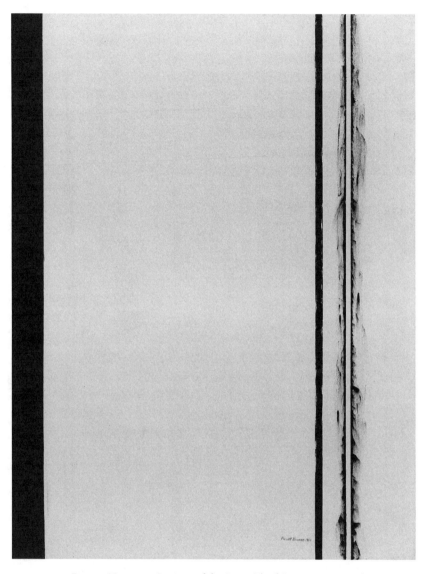

FIGURE 13. Barnett Newman, *Stations of the Cross: Third Station*, 1960. © The Barnett Newman Foundation, Artists Rights Society (ARS), New York / IVARO, Dublin (2015).

FIGURE 14. Barnett Newman, *Stations of the Cross: Ninth Station*, 1958. © The Barnett Newman Foundation, Artists Rights Society (ARS), New York / IVARO, Dublin (2015).

FIGURE 15. Barnett Newman, *Stations of the Cross: Tenth Station*, 1960. © The Barnett Newman Foundation, Artists Rights Society (ARS), New York / IVARO, Dublin (2015).

anticipate and cumulatively express his final anguished cry upon the Cross.[8] Such moments of supreme anxiety may owe their particular intensity to the accumulating significance of previous moments, insights, feelings, and events from the past, even long-forgotten ones. All these factors are woven together in a whole whose structure makes us what we are but whose weaving is not subject to our will.

The spatial structure of Newman's works, then, explores states of mind that lead up to and are implicated in both the meaning of and the answer to Christ's question. In this regard, let us recall that the presumption of virtuality in abstract works leads us to look for some visual symbolic content in them over and above their strictly physical properties, which is provided by the various aspects of transperceptual space. In Newman's work, special importance should be assigned to aspect (3), visual details that suggest things yet without presenting enough familiar aspects to allow their conclusive identification, and to aspect (4), idealized variations on or reductions to features basic to the structure of visual perception, such as mass, volume, density, shape, and color. These formal features in Newman's works are manifest presentations of the transperceptual features just mentioned. His basic spatial format involves a broad zip at the left- or right-hand side with a zip or zips two-thirds of the canvas away from it. This structure goes through various permutations, suggesting a preoccupying thought/feeling that is striving to articulate itself under different aspects.

This articulation is achieved in a different way in each individual work. Of decisive importance here is the character of the ground, the raw white canvas, which in its very rawness and uniformity suggests an ultimate ground that cannot be penetrated. The relation between it and the zips, however, is ambiguous. For there to be perception—and by extension consciousness—there must be, at a minimum, figure recognized in relation to a ground.[9] Newman reduces this relation to its starkest through the simple device of a vertical that can be interpreted, as noted earlier, as physically on top or in front of a ground, or virtually as an incision or gap through which a deeper ground is showing. Like human existence, it is manifestly physical, yet with another aspect emergent from this physicality. Newman evokes thereby a sense of the human subject's relation to being. The raw field is a brute spatiality out of the midst of which we emerge, dividing ourselves off from it through perception and thought. Yet we cannot do so absolutely; our physical aspect is always spatial, and the things we value are likewise infused with spatial criteria, such as their proximity and distance from us.

How, then, does the human subject confront this foundational spatiality? By choosing to work with black and white alone, Newman allows the fundamentality of the encounter to be emphasized through broader associations—for example, between light and dark, being and nonbeing, and so forth. The most important transperceptual association, however, concerns the character of the zips themselves. They may evoke the half-remembered corners of rooms or large windows divided by single panes and the like; but these associations merely express a deeper truth that Newman's visual format extracts and idealizes, namely, verticality itself.

In this regard, it is useful to consider a remark by Merleau-Ponty: "It is no coincidence that the rational being is also the one who holds himself upright. . . . The same manner of being is evident in both aspects."[10] For the human being, verticality is not just a dimension of space; it is the basis of how we engage with space in both physical and cognitive terms. A creature that walks upright can—with a turn of the head—survey the field of spatial things set out in depth all around it and thus comprehend things that are beyond its immediate powers of touch, hearing, smell, and taste. Verticality of posture is basic to our existence as both space-occupying and rational creatures.

This vertical essence of the embodied subject explains why Newman's zips have such visual and aesthetic resonance: they express human spatial orientation in purified terms. But there are several other important aspects to them as well. The first involves the aforementioned areas of formal activity that sometimes play about the zips. In the *First Station*, for example, this activity involves forms that appear to be attempting to cling to the vertical or to attack it; there may even be suggestions of barbed wire or of the Tree of Life with a serpent coiling around it. However, while in this work—and in numerous others in the series—the zip's edges become porous, corroded, and uneven at times, the encroaching elements never pass between the zip and the viewer; the zip has a frontal integrity that is sustained throughout the whole series of paintings.

Now let us consider this phenomenology of the zip's verticality in relation to its ground. This relation has already been described as involving brute spatiality, but what might this mean in more specific terms? Three interpretations may be offered, based on the answers to the ultimate metaphysical question discussed in Section II. Newman himself seems to have favored the existential answer. In these terms, the vertical integrity of the zips or their frequent positioning at the margins of the painting would connote both the inexplicable presentness of human being in space and the states of mind—relating to our isolation and/or abandonment there—that may be consequent upon such placement.

The second, monistic interpretation of the zips' visual and aesthetic resonance would have a different orientation, emphasizing how the zips and the ground create and mutually define and declare one another; one can focus on each of them individually, but in the context of the whole work they are mutually dependent. To emphasize this interpretation is to see each of Newman's paintings in the series as a different way of individually expressing an important metaphysical insight, namely, that the finite subject cannot comprehend the absolute in complete terms, but can at least recognize itself as being an element within that absolute—and indeed a necessary element, without which the absolute would not be complete.

The third, theistic interpretation would have yet another orientation, regarding the vertical integrity of the zip in relation to its ground both as a hopeful presence before God and—in playing its role of declaring the ground—as an acknowledgment of God's presence.

All three interpretations can make the vertical integrity of the zip in relation to the ground metaphysically meaningful in their own terms. This is also true of the ambiguous optical relations between the zip and the ground. As stated previously, we can see the zip as something placed before the ground or as an incision or vertical divide in the surface through which a hidden ground is showing through. A further ambiguity holds by virtue of the relation between zips that are physically painted vertical lines or bands and those that appear as zips through optical effects arising from the relation between these painted verticals or from the painted zip's relation to the raw canvas. (A good example of the latter is in the *Fourth Station*, where a white zip seems to be inscribed in a broader black zip but is actually the raw canvas ground showing through between two thin, black verticals). Each painted zip, in other words, can be seen under different aspects: constituted by its relation to other such zips or to the ground, or both.

Accordingly, our three answers to the ultimate metaphysical question might interpret this oscillating aspectuality of the zip/ground relation as follows. The existential approach would take it to be symbolic of the embodied self's immersion in and overwhelming by the field of space-occupancy. The monist approach would take it as showing that the subject and the whole cannot be separated; each is dependent on the other for its identity. And the theistic interpretation would take the ambiguity to be expressive of the aspiration not only to be present before God but to enter the divine realm and dwell there as one-self in a higher form. There are times when we feel we will take our place there, but at other times we fall away, feeling unworthy and internally divided by pressures on our faith. For Christian theism, indeed, the fact that a zip some-times appears through revelation of the underlying ground may even be taken as the sign of a human subject—Christ—whose subjectivity is of divine origin.

The very fact that Newman's pictures can sustain such different interpreta-tions is of great importance. His work shows a relation between individual sub-jectivity (symbolized by the zip) and a ground—a relation presented as being inherently complex and oscillating, a site of questioning more than explana-tion. This is true to who we are: it is central to the human essence to question ultimate things, but it is equally true of our finite essence that no answer will come in the complete form that we desire. We appear to be forsaken—Christ's final cry speaks, in symbolic terms, for us all, as finite beings.

The cry itself, however, offers an answer of sorts, for in order even to utter it we must recognize meaning. Our idiom of space-occupancy and ways of negoti-ating becoming must be organized around fundamental meaning-creating struc-tures, at the heart of which is the figure/ground relation, the basic and recurrent structure through which space-occupancy is made meaningful. It is this that al-lows us to recognize constants in the flow of becoming, a recognition bound up with the development of rationality; it is integral to every human being who ever existed or will exist, including the embodied Christ. Newman's paintings extract and show this structure—not as a formula of cognition but as a vehicle of tran-scendence. He himself noted that "the cry, the unanswerable cry, is world with-out end. But a painting has to hold it, world without end, in its limits."[11] In these terms, painting is not itself the answer to the ultimate question, but it does allow us at least to merge ourselves with the universal condition of things becoming meaningful, a condition that—in the monist and theistic interpretations—is also the sign of an even greater becoming-meaningful. Newman's *Stations of the Cross* series, then, engages with the mystical sublime in the deepest terms. It addresses metaphysical despair, circumscribed by art's capacity to articulate this and sug-gest the possibility of some more comprehensive redemption.

## IV

Now we turn to the work of Mark Rothko. Like Newman, he achieved his ma-jor artistic breakthrough in the late 1940s, by which time biomorphic surrealist compositions had given way to works characterized by areas of "multiform"

floating color, with no significant biomorphic or other residual figurative elements. By 1951 he had arrived at a basic format for these: horizontal bands
or apparent squares of porous single color, usually upon a different colored
ground. Sometimes these extend from one vertical edge of the canvas to the
other, but they are most often visually framed by the edges of a color field that
seems to extend beneath them. Rothko's ground fields never function as mere
support. They are often finely differentiated and vary in the intensity of their
color saturation from the top to the bottom of the picture; sometimes a field
within the field is created as a second framing structure for the bands. Through
all this, the field actively intervenes on how the bands and their relations to one
another are perceived.

The individual bands themselves involve complex levels of variation in terms
of the density and luminosity of their color. Rothko often creates even more
complex variations on a single color between the bands (often forming a band in
their own right) and in the spaces around their edges. Another familiar device
is the slight darkening or lightening of a small border area within the margins of
the bands, which visually emphasizes their rectangular shape yet without making them appear to us as geometric forms.

This creates, in turn, a very interesting visual dialectic with the actual
boundaries of the bands. With the exception of a few very late works, the band
edges are often frayed and always uneven, even if only to a slight degree. This
means that both the areas between bands and those between bands and the
field or fields are of the greatest visual complexity. The bands are not simply
there as formal structures but involve a subtle optical animation, which has
two major expressions. First, there is a suspension of any straightforward push/
pull opticality (of the sort emphasized by Hans Hofmann) between the bands
and the fields. What Rothko achieves instead is a profound stasis—not in the
sense of mere formal balancing-out but rather in that of arresting a complex of
emergent color/light energies. Second, the relations between the edges of the
bands and the field are invested with a visual homogeneity. Bands and fields
and their zones of connection seem all to be of the same stuff, even though
they have their own individual formal character; they exemplify a kind of
homogeneity-in-difference.

Let us explore all this in relation to an example: *Light Red over Black* (1957)
(Figure 16), which is just over 91 × 60 in. (232.7 × 152.7 cm). The upper black
band is painted in denser terms than the lower one, and the curvature of its four
corners is emphasized in a way that makes it appear more visually compact.

FIGURE 16. Mark Rothko, *Light Red over Black*, 1957. © 1998 Kate Rothko Prizel and Christopher Rothko / Artists Rights Society (ARS), New York / IVARO, Dublin (2015).

The lower band is bigger, however, and has more sustained areas of visual "fraying," especially across its lower edge. This fraying does not weaken its visual impact but rather adds a level of formal interest that compensates for the greater compactness of the upper band. In this painting, then, visual stasis is achieved through qualitative visual features rather than quantitative ones alone. The compositional structure of Rothko's canvases is centered on a highly productive equilibrium. There is an exact calibration of bands and field(s) that makes the bands appear as if hovering, perhaps even as animate entities of a mysterious kind. In *Light Red over Black*, this effect arises from the uneven densities with which paint is applied across the bands, especially the lower one.

In effect, the work involves space-occupying forms that declare becoming-visible. While things become visible all the time, we are generally preoccupied with our day-to-day practical interests to notice this emergence. Any place in which we are presently situated, for example, changes its visual appearance in accordance with the available light sources and the specific character of how they illuminate surfaces and spaces. But if we are washing the dishes or attending to a computer screen or the like, we never think of how things become visible—we have no time for considering such broader meanings. This means, in other words, that everyday life does not favor consideration of how becoming-visible is basic to our experience of space-occupancy. Such becoming is no more than an unnoticed aspect of transperceptual space. *Light Red over Black*, in contrast, draws attention to becoming-visible and in so doing also exemplifies one of the most important aspects of Rothko's mature oeuvre in general.

It is worth dwelling a little more on how this becoming-visible is achieved. The band structure of *Light Red over Black* emphasizes the horizontal dimension of space-occupancy—perhaps better described as the "horizonal aspect." For while the human body is oriented toward the vertical through its posture, the limits of its immediate operations are marked out by the perceptual horizon and the substance of things as spatially extended. Our created spatial environment is dominated by square and rectangular shapes, on the basis of which we fabricate dwelling places and other structures. In Rothko's work, there is a kind of merging of the human spirit with the basic spatial structures of the horizonal in which it lives. The suggestion of spirit is achieved through the aforementioned uneven densities of paint and fraying effects, as well as through the suggestion of veiled luminosity within the bands and fields—a light suggestive of something living and actively working through the human level of space-occupancy.

Now, while the structures just described are basic to Rothko's mature work, he varied them in a number of important site-specific commissions, most notably for the purpose-built chapel in Houston that now bears his name. We shall consider a different set of works, however. In 1958, Rothko received a commission to paint a series of pictures to be hung in the Four Seasons restaurant in the Seagram Building in New York, a commission that caused him many problems but also led him to explore alternative pictorial formats.[12] Even though he withdrew from the commission, he was able to complete three series of works based on it; and between 1968 and 1969 he gave nine pictures (taken, apparently, from the second and third of these series) to the Tate Gallery in London.[13] We shall proceed to discuss a group of them.

The group consists of five works each titled *Black on Maroon* (four of them from 1958 and one from 1959) and four works each with the title *Red on Maroon* (painted in 1959). In all these works, the relation between the band structures and the color field is extremely close, with the transitions and distinctions between the colors sometimes hard to discern. The term "band structures" needs to be used here because of Rothko's variation of his usual format. Three of the *Red on Maroon*s, for example, involve rectangular and vertical red bands that appear to be destabilizing and becoming filamentary against the darker maroon ground. In two of the paintings, the inner horizontal borders of the bands are gently concave. One of the *Black on Maroon* group has a similar structure, but here the black framing area tends to make the central band appear more square than rectangular.

The *Black on Maroon* paintings are each based on two or three vertical black bands that join with a black border to form a barred appearance (Figure 17). In the *Red on Maroon* 1959 version of this format, the effects are more dramatic still (Figure 18): here a dominating rectangular band of ethereal luminous maroon/red is internally differentiated to create the optical effect of an internal opening with light in the distance. The effect is extended through a faint trace of the darker maroon background field left visible in the bottom portion of the band. Hints of it also occur as a thin framing device both outside the limits of the vertical band and within the internal borders of the rectangle of "light." This creates the further optical suggestion of a distant horizon before which, in the immediate foreground, two columnar forms rise up.

Earlier, I suggested that a central effect of Rothko's is the disclosure of space-occupancy becoming visible. The present group of works achieve this in an interesting way. We will recall that aspect (3) of transperceptual space

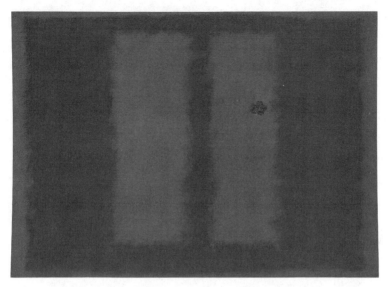

FIGURE 17. Mark Rothko, *Black on Maroon*, 1958. © 1998 Kate Rothko Prizel and Christopher Rothko / Artists Rights Society (ARS), New York / IVARO, Dublin (2015).

FIGURE 18. Mark Rothko, *Red on Maroon*, 1959. © 1998 Kate Rothko Prizel and Christopher Rothko / Artists Rights Society (ARS), New York / IVARO, Dublin (2015).

involves half-remembered details of things we have experienced, suggesting the thing without making it concrete. This is very much the case with Rothko's Tate works, and here indeed we have an important iconographical clue to a transperceptual specific. John Fischer, recalling a conversation with Rothko from the spring of 1959, quotes Rothko as saying, in relation to works included in the Tate group:

> After I had been at work for some time . . . I realized that I was much influenced subconsciously by Michelangelo's walls in the staircase room of the Medicean Library in Florence. He achieved just the kind of feeling that I'm after—he makes the viewers feel that they are trapped in a room where all the doors and windows are bricked up, so all they can do is butt their heads forever against the wall.[14]

These remarks not only provide an example of the half-remembered detail as a formative transperceptual factor but also show its broader significance. For it is neither here nor there if an abstract shape derives from some half-remembered experience or not unless that shape can unlock a specific associational field for the potential viewer. Rothko describes how, in effect, the windows of the Medicean library provide formal structures with claustrophobic associations. They are false windows made of stone and thus offer no vision of the "outside."

Clearly Rothko saw the forms associated with these structures in his work as symbolic expressions of futility and despair. Some important remarks from three years earlier, however, put this in an important qualifying light:

> I'm not an abstractionist. . . . I'm not interested in relationships of color or forms. . . . I'm interested only in expressing basic human emotions—tragedy, ecstasy, doom and so on—and the fact that lots of people break down and cry when confronted with my pictures shows I communicate those basic human emotions. . . . The people who weep before my pictures are having the same religious experience I had when I painted them.[15]

The Tate works are clearly full of tragic and doom-laden associations, but Rothko's remarks here suggest that his art is also concerned with catharsis and religious significance. This links up with the three broad answers to the ultimate metaphysical question that we considered in relation to Newman earlier in this chapter.

To see why, we must first consider their structures in more detail. In what ways do they constitute a making-visible? The obvious place to start is with the restricted, sombre color scheme and the oppressiveness that Rothko identified with it. This might evoke the first, existential answer to the ultimate metaphysical question: we and the world exist without further reason. Yet we must be mindful of the sophisticated visual means of this evocation. Because the structures in the works are mysterious and veil-like in some respects, it is almost as if the paintings function as backdrops in relation to which the spectator introspects. He or she becomes a kind of external figure, achieving self-recognition in relation to the painting as ground.

This, of course, enhances the sense of existential isolation, but insofar as it binds subject and object of perception in an intimate way, it also provides a link to the second, monist answer, namely, the mutual dependency between subject and being. The relative homogeneity of the color schemes also sustains this interpretation, as does the complex aspectuality, in which (as in the relation between Newman's zips and the field) the identity of the bands as either real and painted or just optical effects becomes highly ambiguous. Their individual identity is determined through their role in the whole structure rather than in isolated terms.

The third, theistic answer to the ultimate question is indicated by the way in which the bands and fields hover or vaguely shimmer with the suggestion that the surface appearances take on form and substance through direction from a guiding light beneath the surface. There is a sense that what is made visible is itself the making-visible of a deeper truth. Indeed, the suggestion of veils or uncanny formations of mist reinforces this sense of something even more fundamental hidden beneath.

As in the case of Newman, therefore, it would seem that Rothko's Tate pictures have structures consistent with different metaphysical positions and that the suggestion of these provides an oscillating interpretation—a position moving from one approach to another without definitive resolution. Then why, let us ask again, should this be found pleasurable as well as disturbing? What is the positive aspect of the mystical sublime here? In Rothko's case, what he *does* with the relation between becoming and space-occupancy is decisive. The hovering or dimly shining appearance of his bands suggests momentary states of being, rendered precarious in the flow of becoming. But at the same time, their horizontal or vertical band structure involves extended spatiality, perhaps even the suggestion of monumental form. They appear to stabilize the flow of becoming through their extended mode of space-occupancy.

This produces some extraordinary calibrations. In the Tate pictures, for example, the suggestion of barred windows in some of the *Black on Maroon* works is subverted by their feathery edges; and in the vertically banded works, the monumental columnar structures are nudged toward insubstantiality by their apparent luminosity. Making-visible in Rothko involves space-occupying masses rendered as and through a created moment of becoming: either they are about to change their visual appearance or are changing in microstates below the threshold of perception.

The momentary emerges through the coming into being and passing away of space occupants; it is fundamental to our ordinary states of consciousness in both its presence and its passing but dissolves as soon as we try to catch it. The momentary has that unbearable lightness of being described by somewhere by the novelist Milan Kundera as a terrible gravity of the finite, yet also one that can be considered as wonderfully light when it takes wing through the joy of activity and achievement.

Earlier in this book I argued that pictures intervene upon our experience of the visible and involve an aesthetic transcendence. One aspect of this is an eternalization of the moment. As we saw in Chapter 3, the presentness of the picture appears to suspend the passage of time, while still being emergent from a physical object that is in real time. It is only through such presentness that we can complete ourselves, by simultaneously being in time and transcending it. Rothko's pictures perform a similar eternalization in a highly distinctive way. Their making-visible brings enduring shapes into a visual form in which they hover on the point of dissolution or change. The reciprocity between space-oc-cupancy and becoming is disclosed in aesthetic terms as a universal structure that is the basis of any possible consciousness. A universal structure is some-thing that can be present in an indefinite number of instances, at an indefinite number of places and times, to an indefinite number of observers. When we peer into the abyss of being through art, we do not get something reflected back—we get a transformation into universality and thus transcendence of our finite limitations. Rothko's universalization of the moment is of this order.

Interestingly, Rothko often declared his indebtedness to Nietzsche's *Birth of Tragedy*. What I have been describing here in key respects embodies what he likely found most valuable in Nietzsche's book, namely, the relation between the Apollinian and the Dionysian. The Apollinian is a sensibility that yearns for order and stability and whose essence is to create and give form; the Dionysian, in contrast, is a yearning for change and transformation, a desire to be carried by the tide of fate beyond one's control. The dialectic of visual space-occupancy and becoming allows Rothko to bring these two factors into a profound harmony—the universalizing of the momentary. This is not just a stand-off or balancing out; rather, Rothko's mode of painting is one whose stylistic identity makes the two work together. Through experiencing this harmony, we come to exist in the world in a fuller way.

For those who answer the ultimate metaphysical question in existential terms, this is surely enough. We are tied to finitude and all its despair, but at least we can make our experience of it partially redemptive through immersing ourselves in the reciprocity between becoming and space-occupancy achieved through Rothko's eternalization of the visual moment. The monist will take this further, regarding such aesthetic transcendence as an ultimate fulfilment wherein one experiences the mutual permeation of self-identity and the wholeness of being. The theist, going further still, will find the reciprocity between becoming and space-occupancy experienced as aesthetic transcendence to be meaningful in a deeper sense. For him or her, this eternalization of the moment is itself the image of a higher state of being that is God's gift. This achievement of aesthetic transcendence, indeed, is taken to show how finite beings can participate symbolically in an aspect of divine consciousness. Such achievement is a concrete example of what being made in the image of the Supreme Creator may involve.

## Conclusion

The basic position presented in the latter part of this chapter may be summarized as follows. The mystical sublime is distinguished from other modes of the sublime by the specific ambiguity of its negative aspect, which concerns our sense of place in the universe and the shifting beliefs and doubts through which this ambiguity is embodied. An element of ambiguity applies to some degree to the positive aspect of the mystical sublime as well. For Newman and Rothko this centers on a disclosure of the reciprocity between becoming and space-occupancy. By showing this relation in different visual ways, stylistically speaking, they exemplify a universal level of comprehension involving aesthetical transcendence of some of the limitations of finitude. But by showing such meaning rather than systematically comprehending it in discursive terms, Newman's and Rothko's styles of color-field abstraction cannot be pinned down by one interpretation alone. They offer a phenomenal experience wherein the overwhelming uncertainties of ultimate reality are expressively comprehended through a specific mode of art practice.

The key theoretical implications of this practice have been identified by the theory proposed here. But how—indeed, whether—these implications are relevant at all can only be determined through direct perceptual acquaintance with the pictures themselves. While I have argued that Newman's and Rothko's work is based on universally significant aesthetic insight, the ultimate meaning of such experience is not definitive—not even for the person who has it. In other words, the mystical sublime centers, on the one hand, on a yearning for truth and understanding of our ultimate place in the world and, on the other, on a sense of our limits and fallibilities in this regard. When the relation between these is posited through art, it can be experienced as a reciprocity and not just a tension. Newman and Rothko show this in very special ways through their pictorial explorations of becoming and space-occupancy.

# 5 HOLISTIC BEAUTY
## AT THE LIMITS OF ART
### *Photocollage, Painting, and Digital Imagery*

## Introduction

So far we have considered aesthetic factors based on transcendence—pictorial art's evocation of relations or structures that exceed our finite limitations. Before proceeding to the religious dimension of all this, it is worth considering another possibility: that of a semipictorial art practice that achieves aesthetic completeness through crossing boundaries between visual media. It offers a distinctive form of "holistic beauty" (a term that will be explained a bit later).

The setting for this is very complex in both historical and conceptual terms. It might be said that, since the late twentieth century, the visual arts have reached their creative limits in structural terms. The physical basis of visual art media and the basic semantic and syntactic conventions that govern them cannot be extended further. There can still be original work, but not at the level of large-scale innovation that has driven the great "isms" of Western art.

It might also be argued, however, that a claim of this sort is wholly unwarranted. It is logically possible that some new Masaccio- or Picasso-type genius will emerge and revolutionize the whole artistic enterprise once more. But such a response misses the point: the problem is not a lack of potentially hypercreative humans but rather limits defined by the physical, visual, and referential conventions of visual art media. Even if the geniuses are out there, there is nothing that would allow them adequate expression in terms of far-reaching, structural innovation that would allow art to be done in entirely new ways. In turn, it can be argued that the development of digital art itself offers at least some ways of developing old media as well as fascinating opportunities for new structural developments of its own.[1] If this form of visual art continues to be developed, it might involve radical changes in how art and the artist are conceived. Indeed, it might even be that far-reaching digital innovation takes place alongside the emergence of new technologies that enable artistic innovation or refinement on a scale that parallels or even exceeds the achievement of mathematical perspective.

But even if this art becomes widely influential, it will not be the whole story. The very abundance of digital imagery—especially of an immersive kind—will always call the viewer back to visual artworks that are two- or three-dimensional physical individuals rather than visual tokens of electronic types. Drawings, paintings, and sculptures, for example, are thingly in a way that digital scenarios are not. And for a finite embodied subject, there is a need for examination and stabilization of the self at the level of reencounterable particular material items (and stable interactions between them) that enable the correlated development of self and language.

Pictorial and sculptural art work at this level. Their meaning emerges through being seen rather than being electronically activated and then seen (under mechanically determined conditions). As long as human beings are embodied, the physically individual idioms of visual art will have a continuing ontological priority. This is likely to ensure their survival in the face of any greater innovatory potential opened up by digital art.

Nevertheless, these traditional art idioms do not, in themselves, seem able to sustain the structural development that was the basis of artistic innovation and revolution in earlier eras. Yet this may be for the good. If previously art advanced through refining and extending the structures of its different media, and if that structural potential is now exhausted, then in one respect this might be a sort of liberation. We can regard the history of visual art as a sustained exploration of the structure and scope of the different media; therefore, as we now know what these media are capable of, we can put them to use in new ways. And an obvious first step would be to combine the possibilities of different media in relation to specific projects. In this respect the work of Bracha Lichtenberg Ettinger (discussed in Chapter 3) is exemplary through its use of photocopying and painting as a way of coming to terms aesthetically and morally with the Holocaust.

There are surely many other such projects that cross boundaries between different visual media so as to explore fundamental levels of experience. In this

chapter, I shall propose one such project, which consists of a kind of cooperation between photography, painterly strategy, and digital art. The focus of
attention here is the relation between human experience and the momentary
aspects of Being. This emphasis is warranted not only because the role of momentariness in experience has been relatively neglected, but also because it is
all too easy to think of it as mere fragmentation—which is far from being the
case. Being's momentary aspects are a power of unity in human experience.
Indeed, as I have already argued, visual art's transformations of it into "presentness" are central to why we find such art intrinsically fascinating. In dealing
with the role of photography, however, considerations other than presentness
are involved. Photography does not create the eternalized photographic moment through making it but rather through capturing it; here the momentary's
character is that of a trace. In the remainder of this chapter, then, we shall consider how the experience of momentariness can be illuminated and brought to
a kind of completion through cooperation between old and new media.

I

As a starting point, it is useful to consider some remarks by Jürgen Habermas.
In his celebrated essay "Modernity—An Incomplete Project," he addresses the
issue of how aesthetic experience can be integrated with the life-world. We are
told that

> an aesthetic experience which is not framed around the expert's judgement of
> taste can have its significance altered; as soon as such an experience is used to
> illuminate a life-historical situation and is related to life problems, it enters into
> a language game which is no longer that of aesthetic critic. The aesthetic ex-
> perience then not only renews the interpretation of our needs in whose light
> we perceive the world. It permeates as well our cognitive significations and our
> normative expectations and changes in the manner in which all these moments
> refer to one another.[2]

Habermas illustrates his point by using an example from Peter Weiss' *The
Aesthetics of Resistance*. Weiss describes a group of young workers in Berlin in
1937 who through evening classes acquire a knowledge of the general and social
history of European art. Habermas notes that

> out of the resilient edifice of this objective mind, embodied in works of art
> which they saw again and again in museums in Berlin, they started removing
> their own chips of stone, which they gathered together and reassembled in the

context of their own milieu. This milieu was far removed from that of traditional education as well as from the existing regime. These young workers went
back and forth between the edifice of European art and their own milieu until
they were able to illuminate both.[3]

Even if we interpret "chips of stone" here in both a literal and metaphorical
sense, Habermas' example is not compelling. For to steal chips of stone—or
in the metaphorical reading, fragments of art historical knowledge—and re-
assemble them in a different context is at best a use of art. In such a strategy,
found objects are taken from their high-art context in order to yield broader
existential knowledge. Why this should count as aesthetic experience is, alas,
not clarified by Habermas.

His example does, however, have two positive implications. The first is that
if artistic form is to be a vital element in life-world experience, it must have the
capacity to offer aesthetic illumination of personal and group situations. The
second is the possibility that this can be achieved through the fragmentation
and reconfiguration of the historical continuum. Habermas seems to see this as
a more democratized form of artistic activity. Indeed, it can be; but it does not
have to be in opposition to the more specialized critical judgment.

To see why this is so, let us consider a few points about photography in
general and then undertake a more detailed discussion of one of its uses. Photography is a mode of visual reference that, as noted earlier, is causally rigid.
If the image really is a photograph of the thing it appears to be a photograph
of, then the thing in question once existed. We know this because the image
results from the mechanically registered causal impact of light from the thing
photographed. This causal basis of photography is a simple fact, but it has far-
reaching and complex psychological implications concerning mortality. Every
photograph has the character of the uncanny, inasmuch as it presents that
which has gone into the past in the very act of going into the past.

Now let us consider a tendency in photography that reaches far back into
the last century with the development of photomontage by Man Ray, John
Heartfield, and others. The essence of photomontage is to combine multiple
photographs, as well as other visual material on occasion, in a single image.
This may involve a simple juxtaposition of photographs or the use of cutaway
fragments of prints; in the latter case, we can justifiably speak of "photocollage."

There is a crucial question to be asked about this practice, namely, does it
matter whether the image is derived solely from photographs taken by the artist
in person? The verdict of history so far has been, in practical terms, no. Artists

working in this idiom have, by and large, been willing to use photographs taken both by themselves and by others in composing the final image. But historical circumstances have changed. What if a form of photocollage developed that was founded on the explicit convention that the photocollage must be composed exclusively from photographs—even snapshots—taken by the artist? At first sight this might seem to be an arbitrary stipulation about how photocollage should be done. But while photocollage—like all visual idioms—is predominantly an art of spatial realization, there is also a significant temporal dimension, which in normal photocollage is scattered. We find images taken by different people combining different places and times. If, in contrast, all the combined photographs or fragments thereof are taken by a single individual, what results is a combination of places and times that are moments from the continuum of that individual's personal history. Visual aspects of events in a specific individual's life are thus made into an object.

Accordingly, we might term this form of photocollage the "experience-object." Such objects, in their conjunction of images, might be developed as Heartfield developed his works—to make visual narratives. They might also be explored in a broadly surrealist idiom, wherein the juxtaposition of different images creates narratives that subvert themselves by positing impossible visual states of affairs. But the more the final configuration is composed from fragments cut and configured in different shapes or from photographs disposed so as to mask their figurative content, the more it approximates to the condition of abstract or semiabstract painting. An example of such a work, by Arlo P. Darkly, is shown here (Figure 19). To explain its full significance, however, will require further detailed analysis.

A work of this kind is a painterly absorption of photographs that has a distinctive and remarkable ontology with significant artistic relevance. To understand why, we must first clarify some key characteristics that the experience-object shares with painting as an aesthetic object and then, after linking painting to the holistic structure of experience, describe the experience-object's own special relation to this.

II

In the Introduction, the general character of pictorial beauty was described as involving harmonious unities of parts and whole whose harmony is centered on features distinctive to pictorial media. The projection of a virtual three-dimensional content from a virtual two-dimensional plane is its basis; and its unity is an open one, that is, we need not comprehend the work's unity in any

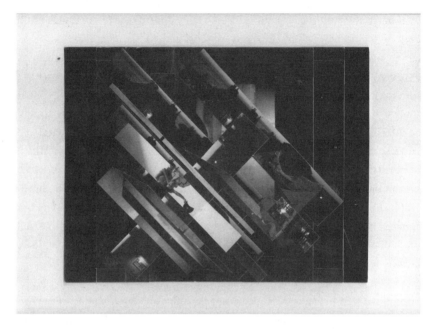

FIGURE 19. Arlo P. Darkly, *The Terminator*, c. 1993. Private collection. Reprinted with permission.

rigid, linear order of succession. The experience-object embodies this pictori-ality in its own modified way. It consists of material pasted on a virtually flat surface that creates a configuration with varying levels of three-dimensional content and having open unity. Insofar as it involves photographs cut and re-assembled so as to create configurations other than visual narratives (of the Heartfield kind, for example) or surreal scenes, it will be meaningful in allusive rather than depictive terms, even though it may contain many recognizable three-dimensional fragments, visually recontextualized.

In these terms, it is clear that the experience-object has a strong affinity with abstract art. We will recall from the previous chapter that such work is generally meaningful through its alluding to transperceptual space. This con-sists of those visual qualities and relations (usually unnoticed) from which the recognizable visual objects of the three-dimensional world are emergent, as well as a network of associations and expectations that are not directly visible but that orient us toward the present visual field. The experience-object's con-figurations will be like this: alluding to hidden visual states of affairs or imag-ined ones, or whatever.

There is, however, one key difference between abstract art and the experience-object. To understand it, we must be guided initially by the notion of the iconographic sublime discussed in Chapter 4, which, we will recall, is operative when our recognition of the negative factor in the dynamic sublime is enabled by iconographic knowledge rather than by what is presented by the immediate visual resources of the work itself.

Iconographic knowledge is also decisive in order for the experience-object to deliver its full meaning. If we do not know that it is composed exclusively from photographs taken by the artist him- or herself, then the work will appear as no more than an abstract work collaged from photographs. But the key point is that in the experience-object, what the artist is composing with are causal traces captured from his or her own visual life history.

If we know this, then our aesthetic exploration of such an object takes on a different emphasis. The traces that the experience-object reconfigures are, in a sense, closer to actual experience than is painting or natural forms. There is a more direct and intimate link to the being of the artist. The events of seeing that he or she has actually experienced—his or her past bodily positionings—are woven into a fabric of new appearance. Painting and other visual aesthetic idioms embody this in a tacit way; the experience-object—inasmuch as we actually know it to be composed from photographs taken by the artist—makes this thematic.

To understand the importance of this, we must now outline (at some length) a complex metaphysical structure that engages with painting (and drawing, of course), which may be called the "holistic structure" of experience. It consists in the fact that no single moment in a human life exists as an isolated, self-subsistent atom, so to speak; it has holistic potency. Any present experience is given its specific character through the reciprocal relation between what is given in that experience and a complex horizon composed of past experiences, our anticipation of future ones, and our counterfactual sense of alternative ways in which our life might have developed.

The individual moment "contains," as it were, the whole of our experience; and reciprocally, with each new moment of experience the character of the horizonal whole is modified. In the passage of life each individual moment is contingent: things in the past might have happened differently, and the way our future will unfold is a developing situation. Once a moment has gone into the past, however, it becomes a necessary part of what we are in the present. Remove or change any moment from a person's past and that person's present and future will also be changed.

This holistic structure is one of the necessary conditions of the human mode of finite self-consciousness and relatedness to Being. It is, however, something we are rarely aware of, except in a philosophical analysis such as this or indirectly, through the arts—most notably through painting. Aristotle famously observed that mimesis holds an intrinsic fascination for human beings; yet he did not point out that the actual process of making is itself intrinsic to this fascination.

As we have seen in earlier chapters, when the painter places brushstrokes on a surface, each new stroke is given its character not only by its own qualities but also by its relation to those that went before it and those future ones that the artist might be anticipating. Reciprocally, this horizontal whole of strokes in place and strokes that might be made is modified by the execution of the present stroke. Of course, areas may be painted over and reworked on the basis of this stroke, but in that case, its significance is changed. The painting over is a causal consequence of this decisive stroke and serves to aesthetically relocate it.

This process, then, exemplifies the holistic structure of experience: the making of a painting in and of itself is a successive series of experiences in a person's life. It embodies and leaves the traces of a holistic structure. These traces, however, are not part of the artist's inner life; they are objectified, that is, rendered in a publicly accessible medium. This gives them a special significance, for it means that the present in which the painting is completed is, in principle, eternalized (as we saw in Chapter 3), along with all those other moments involved in the process of making. The painting marks an episode in the artist's life that has now been brought to completion. Of course, any episode in a life can reach a point of culmination, but it is then absorbed in the ongoing holistic development of that person's life history. In a painting, however, the episode attains a more fully realized completion, in that it is embodied in an artifact that is physically discontinuous from its creator. All the individually contingent moments that informed the work's creation are now rendered necessary, as part of the full identity of the finished work. And since the finished work exists independently of its creator, he or she, as well as the audience, can identify reflectively with this completed structure of experience rather than being immersed in the experiential flow of moments. All those moments otherwise lost in the flux of experience are made into an enduring configuration accessible to others. We have a psychological completion of experience based on the beauty of painting as something made through time.

Painting also manifests the narrative structure of the experiential flow. In applying paint, the artist does so selectively; previously executed areas can be erased or modified on the basis of the present stage of composition. In life, similarly, one comprehends and defines one's present not as the simple consequence of one past moment after another but selectively, as an element in an ongoing narrative wherein some moments of the past are more important than others. Significantly, however, whereas much of one's past is simply forgotten—forgetting being an involuntary act—the artist's erasures and reworking are voluntary; they allow the present to regulate the past volitionally. Thus, the painting is an object of aesthetic pleasure not only in terms of its structures and appearances but also—and in a much deeper way—through its completion and refinement of structures of experience. It redeems what is otherwise lost. It has aesthetic transcendence, as a mode of holistic beauty.

There is, however, a limitation, namely, that the painting's completion of experience is indirect. This is manifest in the way that, historically, painting has been valued for the messages borne by its figurative content or for the beauties of its formal qualities. The aesthetic-phenomenological dimension that I have just identified has scarcely figured in explanations of the nature of our aesthetic response to art. It has not been explicitly articulated as a convention of appreciation. The experience-object goes some way toward rectifying this deficiency. In composing and juxtaposing photographs and fragments thereof, it manifestly exemplifies the structures already alluded to. The photographic material bears direct causal traces of the artist's visual experience; it is, in fact, composed wholly from such traces.[4]

The link with experiential structure here is virtually inescapable and may be taken one step further. In painting, the work is composed in temporally linear terms. Even if one goes back in order to erase or rework, this "going back" is actually metaphorical; literally, however, the erasure or reworking is in temporal terms another stage forward with respect to the previous stages of work. In the experience-object, however, the artist can, if he or she wishes, use images from the distant past of his or her life on top of images from more recent experience. Physically, and in terms of linear time, the images from the far past are in this case more present than the more recent ones. The linear time of the actual process of composition is subverted by the formal assertiveness of material from the distant past. And again this is, in an important respect, true to the narrative structure of experience, for the present is often given its character more by events in the distant past than by more recent occurrences. Even more so than in painting, the temporality of the experience-object is genuinely experiential. Hence, if we know, iconographically, what the experience-object is composed from, then its holistic beauty takes on a slightly different meaning from that of painting itself.

We are left, then, with the following situation. The experience-object uses photographs as if they were the material and means for painting. But it is not painting, nor is it a variety of photography. Rather, it forms a symbolic mode of articulating experience that is inescapably photographic and inescapably painterly, yet reducible to neither. The experience-object is an emergent art form (in every sense) with its own distinctive properties, sustaining a variety of holistic beauty that emerges when we know that it is created from causal traces of the artist's visual experience.

As stated earlier, the experience-object is prefigured by developments in photomontage and photocollage from earlier in the twentieth century. But it has not been systematically worked as a distinctive idiom, one reason for this being the facile progress—or rather, lack of progress—in philosophical aesthetics. A more significant reason is that historical circumstances have only now favored its development, the topic to which we now turn.

## III

Much recent thought has been characterized by a rhetoric of deconstruction that affirms such factors as the instability and transience of meaning, relativity in values, and the decenteredness of the self. Now, at first sight, the experience-object as an artistic idiom would seem to be very much at home in such a context: its very essence involves photographic fragmentation of the linear continuity of experience. As we saw earlier, however, this fragmentation manifests much deeper and more constant structures in perception and experience, to which the experience-object gives its own distinctive inflection. That being said, the experience-object is, in another sense, at least congruent with contemporary skepticism concerning the status of high art, in that it is manifestly *not* a high-art format. Anyone can cut up and reconfigure snapshots so as to create objects with the experiential structures described above.

These considerations suggest that the experience-object would satisfy Habermas' demands of the aesthetic—that it should illuminate personal experience and situations and not be the province of the specialist critic alone. It is vital, however, to emphasize that the experience-object is not antagonistic to a critical-practice culture, for while it is an easily accessible medium, it can be refined and developed—perhaps in surprising ways. Keen-sighted critics could keep abreast of these factors, pointing out repetitions, refinements, and innovations, as well performing more traditional formal appraisals. Indeed, the fact that systematic pursuit of the experience-object as an idiom is new means that the critic is more effectively positioned to carry out these tasks: there is less purely historical ground that has to be mastered.

I mentioned earlier that the experience-object is photographic and painterly but that it is neither photography nor painting. It breaks down the barriers between these in a way that advances itself as a distinctive idiom, yet at the same time illuminates photography and painting. In regard to photography, for example, while the symbolic form of mechanically reproduced representation has been massively developed in the form of filmic, televisual, and video images, that is, in the direction of temporal realization, its development in terms of static, more spatial realization has been somewhat restricted. The experience-object, however, moves us in just this direction; again, through its use of painterly compositional means it illuminates (in ways shown earlier) the experiential structures that inform the act of painting.

Thus we can see that the experience-object is a more accessible medium, yet one that contributes to specialist art practice precisely through overcoming some of the boundaries between two of these practices. This is not some empty formal innovation; by advancing the technical scope of the photo-based pictorial medium, the experience-object also draws upon and articulates constant elements in the historical structure of human experience. It illuminates and transforms the being of subjectivity. Let us now consider some of its further possibilities.

## IV

The analysis so far has centered on the complex ontology of the experience-object. To reiterate: this is a mode of photocollage that consists exclusively of photographs actually taken by the artist. Everything in the experience-object is a mechanically reproduced trace of things that the artist has actually seen. Accordingly, the medium has what might be called an "experiential matrix."

We may now address the question as to what problems and possibilities are opened up if analogies to the experience-object are sought in the realm of electronically based imagery exemplified in technologies other than photography per se. First of all, it is worth briefly considering film, television, and video. These, of course, in contrast to the experience-object, are audio-visual media, that is, art of temporal as much as spatial realization. It is possible nonetheless to operate within them on the basis of an experiential matrix. This requires that the artist work exclusively with material filmed by him- or herself and edit this material unassisted. The result will be episodes or events witnessed or staged by the artist that are then worked up into a new narrative that is more than just the sum of its parts, as well as having intelligibility for a broader audience.

A work of this kind would involve complex interweavings of the documentary and biographical uses of audio-visual imagery and its fictional applications. There are many interesting possibilities here, which it might be possible to develop further through a more detailed analysis of the relation between the notion of an experiential matrix and particular kinds of specialist audio-visual techniques. But this would take us away from the democratizing possibilities of the experience-object, precisely because audio-visual media tend, at least at present, to involve the mastery of complex specialist techniques. This might also seem to be true for those modes of mechanically reproduced or generated imagery based on information technology: what appears to be a specialist practice now may become a commonplace competence within the next few years or so. Nonetheless, it is worth considering some possible variations of the experience-object that are opened up by digital forms of visual imagery. These may be assigned to three basic categories—computer-generated imagery, digital scanning, and virtual reality—that we shall examine in turn.

Computer-generated imagery is a function of specific programs designed by specific people in specific times and places. Suppose, then, that someone sets up visual programs that are meant exclusively as an expression of what we may call the "ambience" of his or her relation to the time and place of programming. Let us also suppose that, at some future point, the programmer is able to variously synthesize these programs and to print out two-dimensional sheets each of which embodies a different configuration of such syntheses.

Now, if the base programs in question here consist exclusively of two- or three-dimensional designs, such programs would not form an exact parallel to the experiential matrix of the experience-object. This is because the base elements of the experience-object consist of photographs taken by the artist, and accordingly have a causal-iconic relation to his or her visual experience. They are isomorphic traces of what was seen. The base programs in the current example, however, do not have this intimate relation to the artist's direct experience; rather, they function as absorptions, interpretations, and expressions of his or her relation to specific times and places of experience. They are thus more analogous to that general horizon of experience which informs creativity in all the traditional artistic media. In effect, what the printouts that synthesize the base programs do is to combine past works of art into new ones.

This, it should be emphasized, is a strategy of significance in its own right. For while artists in any medium can rework old material or combine it with new works, digital media create the possibility of a total synthesis, wherein past programs, designed to be expressive of a particular time and place, can be fused and reconfigured in a new program. The total scope of this integration is distinctively digital, that is, something that is unique to computer-generated imagery. Hence, while this does not form an exact parallel to the experiential matrix of the experience-object, it has an analogous creative dynamic that raises fascinating existential questions in its own right.

It may be, for example, that the total fusion of past and present that it achieves can count as a symbolic overcoming of one aspect of human finitude. In the normal course of experience, there is an opacity in the relationship between present and past; we cannot fully comprehend the way in which past situations inform our present life orientations. In one sense this is all to the good, for if we did not forget the past, individual consciousness would be overwhelmed by the excess of its own history. Yet the disappearance of the past into the forgotten is often described as a loss. The total fusion offered by the digital strategy just described might therefore be understood as a symbolic compensation for this loss. It embodies what in previous chapters has been referred to as an "aesthetic idealization."

While there may be other possibilities opened up by this strategy, let us turn our attention to a much closer relation between digital imagery and the experiential matrix of the experience-object. Here the basic program with which the artist operates is based on the digitalization of photographs taken by him- or herself. It is the experiential matrix translated directly into an electronic medium and opens up two fundamental possibilities.

The first is that of schematic generation. Suppose that the artist scans a huge number of photographs that he or she has taken and makes these into the exclusive basis of a digital visual memory bank. From this, the artist is able to form new programs of visual design that, on the basis of keyboard instructions, are generated only on the basis of visual information contained in the memory bank. Now if, for example, the artist enters a "red sphere against a blue background," the visual configuration thus generated will not correspond to any specific red sphere against a blue background that the artist has photographically recorded. Rather, it will be a schema abstracted from all the elements of shape and color that are contained in the memory bank. It will be an image electronically generated so as to satisfy a linguistic description. The configuration will be specific—red sphere against blue background—but its realization, its particular dimensions and characteristics, will be a function of the idiosyncrasies of the photographic material contained in the memory bank. This means that if two different artists using two different experiential memory banks issue the same keyboard instruction, the result will be two configurations that are the same in terms of the kind of image that is generated but very different in terms of more specific visual characteristics.

This, indeed, is how the imagination functions within self-consciousness itself. Images can be generated so as to satisfy descriptions, but their more particular quasi-sensory characteristics are directed by the experiential history of the individual subject. The schematic-electronic generation of visual images, however, allows something of this individual character to be exemplified at a public level. It enables, albeit in an admittedly restricted way, the communication of the artist's imaginative style.

How significant this possibility is in more general artistic terms is unclear. It is certainly of philosophical interest insofar as it discloses important aspects of the structure of imagination, but then, so do the visual arts per se. Rather than pursue this digital possibility any further, therefore, let us now consider the second avenue of creativity opened up by the photo-based memory bank, which constitutes, in effect, a digital version of the experience-object. Here the artist is able to draw on any of the images in the experiential matrix / memory bank and project them on-screen. Regular or irregular shapes can, as it were, be cut and pasted upon other elements within the digitally projected photograph(s). In contrast to the photographic experience-object, however, there is a range of further technical operations that are easily accessible to the artist. He or she can, for example, dilute or exaggerate colors and magnify, distend, or distort selected areas of the image.

These operations raise several interesting questions. First, the photographic experience-object involves exclusively physical interventions on the material used; one merely cuts up and reassembles prints that are causal-iconic traces of actual visual experiences. Those technical operations described just above in relation to the digital version, in contrast, involve modifications of the photographic image itself. The causal-iconic traces are not simply physically rearranged in relation to one another but rather admit of an additional dimension of qualitative transformation in terms of color, shape, and texture. Then the question is whether this amounts to a qualitative transformation of the ontological structure of the experience-object, and the answer is yes. Through these technical operations the experiential matrix is rendered impure in a positive sense. Its photographic elements are interpreted and transformed on the basis of present interests. This actually overcomes one limitation of the purely photographic experience-object, for the life of memory in the embodied subject does not involve the mere retrieving and connecting of faded images but a creative regeneration of them in the present. The digital technical operations just described are exemplifications of this creative orientation.

There is a further question raised by this digital version of the experience-object. Given the appropriate technical expertise, an artistic photographer can develop prints and manipulate negatives in a way that can achieve effects similar to those created through digital technical operations. Does this mean, therefore, that the difference between the photographic and digitally scanned experience-object is one of degree alone, that is, that it is simply a great deal easier to perform creative alterations by using a computer than through the physical transformation of photographic prints and negatives?

This is a difficult question. It does seem prima facie that the difference here is simply one of degree. But one must also bear in mind the way in which this difference informs the actual process of creation. Photographic transformations take a great deal of time and would, as it were, displace the creative process in spatio-temporal terms. As well as cutting and handling prints and negatives directly, the photographer would also have to spend a lot of time in the laboratory and darkroom in order to achieve the desired effects. And if the compositional results were not satisfactory, the whole arduous process would have to be repeated. In this way the creative process would become disjointed and episodic.

In terms of the final work, if the experience-object so achieved is of great compositional merit, this disruption may not matter. But in another respect it matters very much indeed, because much of the special significance of the experience-object is bound up with the relation between its experiential matrix and the process whereby this is reconfigured into a new formal structure. Process, as well as form, is part of the distinctive code whereby the experience-object can be read as disclosing narrative structures in human experience. In view of this, one might say that the accessibility offered by digital technological operations involves a qualitative difference from the purely photographic experience-object. The fact that they can be deployed directly at the point of contact with the emerging configuration means that the body's relation to the work is more continuous. The artist creates his or her work only through an immediate physical relation to the screen and keyboard. It may be, of course, that this process undergoes many interruptions, but the point is that—in contrast with the achievement of photographic special effects—these disruptions are not integral to the creative process itself.

This continuity of the creative process is actually of broader ontological significance. Whereas in the narrative of experience itself there are necessarily gaps in terms of memory, these gaps do not mark episodes in which the subject ceases to exist; there is continuity in all our experience, provided by the body. This dimension of continuity is symbolized by the digitally scanned experience-object (as well as by painting and drawing) through the continuity of the body's presence in relation to the emerging on-screen configuration.

If this analysis is correct, then it means that the experience-object based on the scanned experiential matrix is distinctively digital, that is, it has something that the purely photographic version does not. This is also true of the third major category of digital imagery, namely, virtual reality. Earlier we noted how parallels to the experience-object in TV, film, and video are possible but are inhibited by the specialized technical knowledge that is involved. We also speculated that, while this is also true of digital imagery to some degree, the accelerating pace of accessibility in that realm is likely to facilitate rapid democratization. There is no intrinsic reason why this should not also be the case for even as complex a technology as virtual reality.

Now, the digital version of the experience-object that we have just discussed is two-dimensional in physical structure; virtual reality (VR) programs take us beyond this into the realm of three dimensions and more. In this regard, let us suppose that an experiential matrix is scanned from video input. This opens up the possibility of a VR program that not only creates a new narrative from past audio-visual experiences but is also a total-immersion environment with complex interactive possibilities.

One aspect of this deserves particular emphasis. Standard immersion in virtual reality creates the illusion of having a second body—in cyberspace. This illusion is the source of much excited speculation, since it seems to involve some transcendence of the real body.[5] But no matter how fantastic or complex VR programs may be, their structure and content are defined by the needs and desires of the real body. Hence, the standard immersion experience involves a double illusion: on the one hand, there is the recognized illusionary transcendence of the body; on the other hand, there is occupancy of a virtual space of events and states of affairs whose significance is—without its being recognized—a function of the real body's desires.

In the VR experience-object, however, matters are somewhat different. Here the virtual space is generated from the experiential matrix, which means that the total-immersion environment is constituted from audio-visual traces of the artist's past. The space that envelops him or her is not a denial of the real body's relation to the world but rather a virtual reinterpretation of it. Indeed, the very fact that the realm of imagery and the experienced world of audio-visual perception here intersect explicitly is a symbolic expression of that reciprocal dependency between imagination and knowledge of self and the world that is fundamental to embodied subjectivity.

Moreover, the additional fact that this relation can be modified interactively serves to deepen the expression of this reciprocity. Virtual reality, in other words, has distinctive ways of disclosing experiential structure. Jos de Mul has rightly observed that in general, "what distinguishes VR programs from older forms of representation such as painting or film is that they do not so much refer to a real world beyond the representation, but constitute another type of being-in-the-world."[6] The VR experience-object, however, is distinctive precisely because it incorporates the real *within* the virtual. It is an aesthetic idealization of our subjective relation to Being.

## Conclusion

In this chapter we have considered the aesthetic potential of the experience-object as a reconstitution of fragments of experience as preserved in photographic traces. The experience-object can be regarded as the basis of a new minor convention of artistic practice, with its own distinctive aesthetic-ontological structures. These structures illuminate both the narrative basis of embodied experience and specific aspects of photography and painting as artistic practices. They disclose and transform the holistic structure of our experience of Being, expressing it in the beauty of an allusive configuration. We are often aware of how our present experiences depend on the past, but in the experience-object this is made into an immediately accessible holistic beauty. Beauty of this kind amounts to a kind of ultimate self-possession for the artist, as well as for his or her audience insofar as such aesthetic and metaphysical completeness is something they aspire to.

We have also considered ways in which the experience-object might be developed in the sphere of new technologies through the use of a photo or video matrix. In particular, we identified ways in which these variants of the experience-object offered distinctively digital articulations of it, that is, creative factors that did not simply duplicate and could not be duplicated by the creative techniques of other art media.

It is important to emphasize this because a great deal of contemporary discussion of the new technologies involves an overrhetorical assertion that "new realities" are being brought into play. In fact, "realities" are not at issue: what *is* at issue are the structure and scope of the symbolic forms that the new technologies embody. It is only when the nature of the medium is carefully thought through in relation to what is distinctive to it that it can be put to genuinely creative use. This is also true of the future of art in general. At present the art world's dominant ideology is one that attempts to ratify anything that the artist chooses to call art, which has the effect of reducing art to mere idea or theory and, in consequence, of turning it over to direction by the managerial sphere.

If art is to advance beyond this dominion, it will only be through the use of different art media to illuminate specific aspects of our relation to Being. This does not involve some rhetoric demanding the collapse of boundaries between different visual art media; rather, it emphasizes the exploration of what is distinctive to one medium in the context of features that are distinctive to others. In this way art can advance—not by way of a search for new revolutionary innovations but by the deployment of what has already been achieved to illuminate more personal and intimate aspects of our relation to Being. The experience-object is one such possibility; doubtless there are many others.

# 6  PERSPECTIVE AND ICON

*Jean-Luc Marion's Theology of Painting*

## Introduction

Throughout this book we have seen how important aesthetic experiences (such as ideal and metaphysical beauty and the varieties of the sublime) can be read in both secular and religious terms. In the final two chapters, we shall consider the religious aspect in more critical detail. The work of philosopher and theologian Jean-Luc Marion provides a useful starting point, since he finds philosophical reasons for assigning special religious significance to pictorial art. Indeed, his theory is also of considerable interest insofar as he is one of the few contemporary thinkers to assign a privileged role to perspective.

Let us begin with an overview of Marion's key operational concepts. He claims that the contemporary world is swamped by images that have become autonomous. This is not a positive phenomenon: according to Marion, the image no longer communicates that which it is an image of but rather exists merely to satisfy the viewer's desire for pleasure for its own sake. As far as I can tell, it is to further understand and deal with the conditions of this malaise that Marion is led to a theology of painting.

He affirms explicitly that this must be a phenomenological account, because painting is an exemplar of visibility and therefore of phenomenality in general. To engage with painting requires not a "return to things themselves" but rather the seeing of what "gives" itself in perception.[1] In this context, for Marion "theology becomes . . . an indispensable authority concerning any theory of painting."[2] The reason for this (as becomes apparent in the course of his account) is that Marion takes the visible world—insofar as it is a world—to be dependent on the "invisible," in both epistemological and metaphysical terms.

For Marion, the key to the invisible is the complex set of interrelations between perspective, the significance of the gaze, the unseen, and in the final analysis, the theological significance of all this. He holds that in the context of painting's historical development, the complex factors in the relation have been articulated in increasingly problematic ways. These difficulties can only be overcome through a renewed understanding of the icon and the theological meaning of the invisible.

## I

Marion assigns great importance to perspective, understood in an unexpectedly broad sense. For him, perspective is the systematic ordering of space in experiential terms. It is the principle whereby we can recognize the systematic arrangement and connectedness of spatial items and states of affairs. As he puts it: "This operation of perspective, which simply opens up the space of things as a world, is accomplished in a way that depends upon the ideality of space, more real than real, since it is the condition of possibility."[3] The latter parts of this remark are of decisive significance. Our experience of spatial depth is not merely the result of a basic coordination between our body and things but is explicitly informed by dimensions of space understood as integrated vectors of potential activity. Whereas an animal can perceive and negotiate depth in a regular way through instinct and habit, in humans depth is experienced as a systematic unity—as spatially ideal.

This ideality of space—or "perspective" in Marion's terms—is an a priori condition of the very possibility of experience. It is an "invisible" factor that makes the visible visible through its cognitive directing of the human subject's explorations of the physical world. Perspective "provokes depth" by projecting "outside the flat plane," that is, by systematically articulating real three-dimensional forms and relations from the two-dimensionality of the retinal image. This, of course, is not a passive beholding; to see a visible world is to know that one occupies a position within it as one spatial object among others, some of which, like oneself, have the capacity to project possible changes in movement and position.

For Marion, perspective in the sense just described is the basis of the gaze. Our perception of the world, together with the significance of the things in it, is oriented by perspective. We see by virtue of perspective, but we do not see perspective itself; it is invisible. This is likewise true of the more subjective or affective lining of the gaze; when we look at someone's face, or for that matter, when they look at ours, what is seen is "not the visible face of the other, an object still reducible to an image (as the social game and its make-up demands), but the invisible gaze that wells up through the obscurity of the other's face; in short, I see the other of the visible face."[4] In these terms, in other words, the other person's face is the site of the gaze. But the perspectival and existential ordering that constitutes the gaze and that, indeed, defines the character of the face (and thus counts as its "other") is not the kind of thing that can itself be made visible. We see an expression of the gaze through the face, but we cannot see its full distinctive mode of being.

Marion also emphasizes that because perspective is invisible, this yields a paradox. In his words, "the visible increases in direct proportion to the invisible. The more the invisible is increased, the more the visible is deepened."[5] HIs point here (one presumes) is that the more invisible (ideal) perspectives we bring to bear on the world, the more our experience of its character as visible is enriched. The visible becomes deeper in both a literal and metaphorical sense. In relation to painting this paradox is doubled. A painting is physically flat, but the relation between the visible and the invisible opens up a world, with a proportionality determined by the depth of perspective. In some cases, such as Turner's *The Pass of Mount St. Gothard* of 1804, "it manifests, directly and uniquely, depth itself, in its unreal, almost complete abstraction."[6]

As one might expect from such a comment, Marion is also willing to link perspective to abstract works. He considers the example of so-called op art, in which abstract forms are distributed and repeated with a visual intensity of rhythm to such a degree that illusions of movement may occur when looking at them. As I understand him, he takes the distribution and repetition involved here to serve an idealizing, "perspectival" function, inasmuch as two-dimensional form is organized in a systematic way so as to generate a level of unstable illusion. Of such art Marion remarks that "the invisible destabilizes the visible in order to contradict the gaze—in order to put itself in movement, therefore, thanks to the immobility of the painting, that it might be seen. This ruse of the visible testifies to the complete ideality of the visibly structured spectacle."[7]

This is not just a point about op art. Here Marion transposes onto painting the paradox already noted in relation to natural vision—that the visible increases according to the measure of the invisible; the perspectival ideality of space makes visible reality possible. While the real space of visible reality can be physically traversed, however, that of the picture cannot. In the picture, perspective closes off the dimension of the picture's flat physical reality through staged levels of illusionistic detail. It "mundanizes a real visible by an infinite number of irreal visibles, and thereby renders the visible all the more apparent."[8]

Marion summarizes his approach (with some nods toward Husserl) in terms of the following "conceptual operation"—which applies both to visible reality and to painting. It consists of three aspects: (1) a real object registered through lived experience; (2) intentionality, in the sense of "invisible" perspectival interpretation; and (3) the completely interpreted intentional object organized in depth and space.

Now, it is clear from all this that while perspective is invisible, in painting we at least have some visual sense of it. It stops us from seeing the painting as just a series of marks on a plane surface, and its pictorial space is organized in a way that suggests various levels of depth. There is a kind of positive equilibrium between the visible and the invisible (though Marion does not put it in exactly these terms). But as we shall see in the next section, this equilibrium undergoes significant transformations when it comes to painting considered as an art.

## II

While the invisible—in the sense of perspective and the gaze—cannot be made visible in every respect, there is an aspect of it that can. This is the "unseen," which comprises things that are hidden but can, under the right circumstances, become visible. Artistic creation is of this kind; it has its origins in the unseen. For example, as Marion observes:

> When El Greco or Caravaggio represent[s] in outline or sketch, of course they do not reproduce any outline, any face previously available in the field of the visible. Nor do they invent arbitrarily. They content themselves with recording the trace that imposes the unseen from its own force. . . . The lines and shapes mark the traces that have never before been sketched, traces of what has never before passed there, visible traces, not of an anterior visible, but of the unseen as such—traces of the invisible.[9]

According to this view, the artist is in effect motivated by the unseen. This does not mean some already worked out idea that only needs rendering in paint in order to become visible. In this regard, Marion tells us that "the whole mastery consists, precisely, in ultimately letting the unseen burst into the visible by surprise, unpredictability."[10] Indeed, "the truly creative painter . . . is characterized not by a plastic inventiveness imposing his will but rather by a passive receptivity, which from a million equally possible lines, knows to choose the one that imposes itself from its own necessity.[11]

In the context of art, then, the unseen is the logic of intuitive choice in terms of what the painter puts on the pictorial surface. Inspiration rather than execution is the key—knowing exactly which choice to make. Marion describes these choices (if I understand him correctly) as "ectypes" or "internal impressions."[12] As the painting develops, its "background" or "fund" of accumulated marks is modified by an ectype—a creative insight that leads the artist to place a new mark or set of marks that modifies the character of the accumulating whole.

There is one feature of this revelation of the unseen that Marion emphasizes again and again:

> The painting—the authentic one—exposes an absolutely original phenomenon, newly discovered, without precondition or genealogy, suddenly appearing with such a violence that it explodes the limits of the visible identified to that point. . . . He deepens a seam or fault line, in the night of the inapparent, in order to extract, lovingly or more often by force, with strokes and patches of color, blocks of the visible.[13]

Authentic painting, in other words, is *original*—it makes visible something the like of which was not visible before, and does so in a way that could not have been predicted. This criterion of authenticity, in effect, separates artistic painting (though again Marion does not make the point explicitly) from paintings that are just produced formulaically, so as to visually illustrate some broader informational content. Authentic painting engages us as art, whereas the other mode does no more than tell us about visible things.

Matters are complicated, however, by Marion's very critical interpretation of key aspects of modern art. He strongly implies that some of its tendencies have lost that dynamic relation of originality and unpredictability which characterizes authentic art. To understand why, it is worth returning to the three-aspect "conceptual operation" that Marion takes to be basic to painting. As we will recall, this comprises the painting as a lived sensory experience, the intentional (perspectival) ordering of this experience, and the intentional object (in effect, figurative or illusionistic content) that is emergent from this. According to Marion, this operation has two axes between which a tension exists. This tension marks out, indeed, the two logical extremes of painting, which are reached when the intentional object or the lived sensory experience is collapsed into the intentionality of perspective itself, thus serving to make the invisible at least partially visible.

In regard to the former extreme (the intentional object), he considers one of Monet's paintings of Rouen Cathedral: "Here, the point is not to see, across this excess of light, the intentional object of a cathedral; it is a matter of receiving this light itself, as perceived, in the place and at the place of all illuminated objectivity."[14] In Monet's picture, in other words, the organizational (light-based) means of rendering the visible is itself made visible. It merges with the lived sensory experience of the painting and thus deposes the intentional object. Visible objectivity disappears from the visible and is replaced by objectification of the means of invisibility itself.

The action painting of Jackson Pollock develops this objectification to the point of disappearance. "The painting consciousness becomes to itself alone, without space or invisible, without intentionality or object, a world. And thus only that. The world of intentional objects dies in the action of painting, which already accomplishes a world in itself."[15] Marion also links this to performance art, in which it is the act itself—the performance as lived sensory experience—on which everything converges. Such work absorbs even its own intentionality without remainder.

Perspectival painting may also disappear from the opposite direction—by eliminating not only the intentional object but also the quality of lived sensory experience. Marion considers Hantai's *Tabula Rasa* (1974), where the dimension of insistent repetition quickly tells the gaze that there is nothing significant to see:

> It is a matter of a minimum visible; the white rows accentuate the blue squares automatically, without my gaze intervening, except to note its delayed vision. The reservation and insignificance of the visible guarantees that it has an autonomy with respect to every experience of consciousness, a consciousness reduced to observing what it no longer constitutes.[16]

Thus, in Hantai's painting and in minimalist works in general, the invisible perspectival organizing factor is simply realized in terms of the visible arrangement of two-dimensional forms. This visual poverty confuses and distresses consciousness, to the point that it cannot exercise the invisible in substantial terms. We find painting without an object in any sense. Even before Hantai and minimalism, this tendency had already been radicalized in Malevich's suprematism. Marion describes the *White Square*, for example, as "the pure thing, issued from nothing other than its own invisibility, literally issued from nothing, in complete independence of states of consciousness, whether of that of the spectator or that of the painter."[17] In such a work, "the visible is liberated from vision at the moment when it seizes its own invisibility. The invisible, from that point on, plays no longer *between* the aim of the gaze and the visible, but rather, contrary to the gazing aim, *in* the visible itself—and is merged with it, inasmuch as the white square is merged with its white base."[18] In other words, whereas the gaze's normally invisible perspectival logic organizes the visible and makes it become visible, in the suprematist painting the gaze's striving for such structured visibility is flattened out in the bare visible of the white square on the white ground. We have the gaze and the logic of invisibility as a mere striving—caught between a minimal visible in which it is inertly manifest and the ghost of an intentional object that has been eliminated entirely.

The upshot of all this is that in such painting, the visible and the invisible are in a state of permanent display. In effect (though Marion himself does not put it quite like this), the visible and invisible are trapped within one another in a way that inhibits our experience of them. For Marion this represents a decline, in that through it painting has lost its authenticity in two respects: "On the one hand, the painting limits itself to being a mere recording, simply recording the most fitting private impressions or spectacles for the desiring gaze, like so many experiences of consciousness being set forth, in order to be read, indeed, on the support and the surface."[19] He continues: "This line of development is seen from Monet to Pollock through Matisse and Masson, and it is precisely this path that leads the way into the impasse of action painting and performance art."[20] On the other hand, "thanks to the painting, the experience is created in which there is no longer anything to see. . . . The visible thus sinks in the conception."[21] As a way out of this two-way impasse, he champions the ontological potency of the icon, the topic to which we now turn.

## III

It should be emphasized, first, that by "icon" Marion does not mean art with figurative content per se but "icon" in its more specific sense, the representation of a religious figure (though, as we shall see later, he does allow that some secular art can share aspects of the icon's ontological richness). Now, according to Marion, the icon involves a distinctive ontology in three key respects. In order to understand them we must first recall that for him, the "gaze" is invisible. It is our mode of address to visible things that interprets them as a logic of the spatial. We can see ourselves or other people gazing, but we cannot see the logic of spatial interpretation and organization that operates in this gaze. Nor, for that matter, can we see the vectors of feeling and personal meaning that simultaneously invest the spatial sense of the world with existential significance.

With this in mind, let us consider Marion's three-aspect account of the icon. The first aspect consists in the fact that, according to him, the icon offers itself to be seen by the gaze without utilizing perspective. Insofar as he has already argued that perspective is the basis of depth perception in general, this is a puzzling claim, to say the least. It may perhaps be explained by the second aspect of the icon—namely, that it always presents a gaze belonging to a human face. A religious figure gazes in response to the gaze of the beholder. And through this, "the icon liberates the image from the mimetic rivalry between the visible and the invisible."[22]

This is one of Marion's most interesting claims for the icon. He emphasizes that the figure represented is a "prototype." Initially, this is considered in terms of the Cross presenting Christ's crucifixion:

> The cross indeed accomplishes first and perfectly the trait that distinguishes a type from, for example, an image: it does not reproduce its original according to degrees of similitude but rather refers itself paradoxically to a prototype more indicated than shown. . . . Christ, on the Cross, holds no more than a typical relation, outside of similitude or dissimilitude with himself.[23]

We do not know how Christ and the cross on which he was crucified actually appeared. There is no original with which we can compare any of our representations of this event. All we have is a "prototype"—a type that every represented cross alludes to but that cannot be made visible in any historically exact way. The prototype (one presumes) is Christ in his spiritual reality. This is, of course, perfectly congruent with the religious meaning of Christ's crucifixion, which requires us not to fixate on Christ's finite corporeal status but to move beyond it to the invisible real of divine being.

As I understand him, Marion generalizes this as a characteristic of the icon as such, a generalization that is broadly consistent with the official theory of the icon in the Orthodox Christian tradition. The religious figure represented in such a work addresses us with his or her gaze, but we have no way of verifying whether this gaze is presented in historically verisimilitudinous terms, visually speaking, because the figure in question can no longer be seen. Yet this is precisely the icon's virtue. We cannot test it against visible actuality; all that we can focus on is the imagined gaze. Through our sense of the prototype, in other words, we are forced from the visible to the invisible power of the gaze that addresses us through the icon.

The more decisive fact, however, is that the gazes of the viewer and the prototype are not left alone with one another, as it were, in a wholly imagined crossing. They converge on the gaze of the figure as painted in the icon. The painted gaze transfigures its own invisibility by emerging as a transformation of the two invisible gazes that it mediates. As Marion puts it, in the icon "the invisible is neither devoted to itself, nor devoted to the surface of the visible, as in perspective. On the contrary, it is the visible that serves the invisible."[24]

This leads to the ironic significance of the third main aspect of the icon: it suppresses its own visibility in more radical—yet more positive—terms than even the suprematist square. For whatever its minimal strivings, the suprematist square is nevertheless still seen. The icon, in contrast, "definitively withdraws itself from the objectivity of a spectacle dependent upon consciousness, by overturning the relation between the spectator and the spectacle."[25] Indeed, as Marion also suggests, "before the profane image, I remain the viewer unseen by an image that is reduced to the rank of an object (the aesthetic object remains an object) constituted, at least in part, by my gaze."[26] With the icon, in contrast, "it is necessary to venerate, that is, by my gaze, to climb back up to cross the visible image and be exposed to the invisible counter-gaze of the prototype. The icon is given not to be seen but to be venerated, because it thus offers its prototype to be seen. The icon is crossed by the veneration of my gaze in response to a first gaze."[27]

As I read him, then, Marion holds that while the modernist tendencies he has described collapse the visible into an inert lived sensory experience, the icon resists this. It is visible but does not exist to be seen as an aesthetic object; rather, it refers us back to the invisible gaze of the prototype. The icon's own visibility is self-suppressing so as to affirm the invisible without collapsing into the realm of mere spectacle. In this way, the invisible is evoked from the visible through the dynamic crossing of gazes that is intrinsic to the icon. The icon has an authenticity that other idioms of painting do not.

This contrast extends even to the idiom of painting to which the icon might seem to be most closely related, namely, the portrait. According to Marion, most portraits treat the gaze of the model as a visible object and arrange it in a perspectival context of dignity and worldly trappings. The icon, in contrast, "removes the prestige of the visible from its face, in order to effectively render it an imperceptible transparency, translucent for the counter-gaze. The icon does not expect one to see it, but rather gives itself so that one might see or permit oneself to see through it. . . . It withdraws from the invisible evidence that it nevertheless reveals."[28]

Marion further suggests that in giving itself up so as to return us to the prototype, the icon hints at Christ's relation to God. This is of the utmost significance. God is "the invisible par excellence,"[29] that is, the organizing power who sustains all existence, including that perspective whereby the world of experience is organized. In this context, icons of Christ have a very special importance. As Marion observes, "I look, with my invisible gaze, upon a gaze that envisages me; in the icon, in effect, it is a matter not so much of seeing a spectacle as of seeing another gaze that sustains mine, confronts it, and eventually overwhelms it."[30] Christ, however, is not, the supreme sustainer of all things; he requires us to love his Father through him: "We thus come to understand how Christ Jesus offers not only a visible image of the Father who remains invisible but even a (visible) face of the invisible itself (the Father), a visible image of the invisible *as invisible*."[31]

## IV

The time has come to critically review Marion's complex theory of painting. We shall begin by developing some of its strengths. A useful starting point is his broad use of the term "perspective" as a synonym for the ideality of space as such. This is rather at odds with customary usage, which applies it specifically to the mathematical organization of pictorial space. Marion's usage is rendered especially awkward by the fact that he even links it to the binocular character of vision[32] despite the fact that perspective in its pictorial form involves orthogonals converging on a single vanishing point, that is, has a monocular structure.

Marion's unconventional usage can be justified, however. The systematic nature of space is ideal—not just in some abstract sense (as an object of scientific knowledge) but in more primal experiential terms. The visible is only visible insofar as space is understood as an ideal system of places and positions that can extend in all directions. Its ideal character is not abstract in the first instance but rather something we know and act on. It is the experienced unity of our motor engagement with things and places, a concrete unity that helps sustain all our perspectives upon the world—be they perceptual or personal.

Marion links his notion of perspective to Nietzsche's "perspectivalism" so as to emphasize its concreteness. But while we might allow him this emphasis, is not the notion of ideal systematicity completely at odds with the substance of Nietzsche's own, more subjectively oriented sense of perspective? Marion shows that it ought not to be. For while individual perspectives upon the world can be just that, the having of perspectives in any sense whatsoever logically presuppose knowledge of the systematic character of space and the agent's role within it. If we did not have the capacity to negotiate space as a systematic unity, then the more specific content of the gaze—as an expression of race, gender, class, personal viewpoint, or whatever—would not get any purchase. (Nor, for that matter, would viewpoints objecting to the possibility of such unity!)

It might be thought that this awareness is culturally specific to the West. But even to experience the world as, say, an unfathomable and unstable place of effects wrought by the spirits actively presupposes that we are perceptually anchored in a world that allows the formation of such interpretations. We need knowledge of space's ideality, however crude the recognition might be. If our prereflective cognitive activity were not habitually guided by this insight, there would be no distinction between human and animal perception. But humans have perspectives on the world. This means choices of action determined not simply by immediate stimuli but by explicit recognition of the nature of space, our relation to it, and what this relation allows and disallows in both physical and broader existential terms. In other words, perspective, in Marion's sense, is a primal orientation; it is integral to our sense of being human.

Marion's link between perspective and the experience of spatial ideality has a second advantage that is an advance on Merleau-Ponty. Merleau-Ponty is highly critical of "classical perspective" in pictorial space, arguing that it involves a disembodied, static, and monocular view of things that is at odds with the dynamic character of our actual perceptual immersion in the world. His critique is deficient, however, in that it overlooks the systematic character of how body and world are correlated, as well as the fact that—within the constraints of a three-dimensional virtual space projected from a two-dimensional planar base—classical perspective is the only adequate expression of this systematicity.

Now, it is clear that Marion's usage of "perspective" emphasizes the systematicity of the body-world correlation in a way that Merleau-Ponty's does not. And by rectifying this deficiency, it means that perspectival painting runs no danger—as it does in Merleau-Ponty—of being hierarchically subordinated to more modern work. Marion's account, however, might appear to run the opposite risk, that of privileging more traditional idioms over modernist work. In this regard, we will recall his negative assessment of some modernist tendencies, such as action painting and minimalism. Fortunately, while Marion is critical of these movements, it is in terms of their specific character; both tend, as it were, to "de-nature" the invisible through absorbing it into the mere act of painting (in the case of action painting) or locking it into a banal display of physical presence. At the same time, he is positive about other modern tendencies such as Duchamp's ready-mades and *arte povera*, inasmuch as these involve "a systematic impoverishment of the spectacle offered to the gaze by the work." By so doing, they reinstitute the importance of the invisible as a factor in painting.[33]

And just as Marion's critique of modernism is selective rather than unwarrantedly global, so too is his approach to perspectival works. He is, for example, critical of paintings that do no more than present a spectacle to vision. Such works denude the vital role of the invisible and the reciprocity of gazes that is found in "authentic" painting. This is even true of most religious art of the twentieth century, where, according to Marion, we are now more interested in the beauty of the image than what the image refers us to.[34]

We shall return to the question of religion and painting. For the present, let us grant that Marion has at least restored perspective in painting to a position of general equality with other idioms. But now we must approach the areas of his theory that are deeply problematic. They all converge on his general theory of the invisible, which, we will recall, takes the term to encompass perspective, the gaze, the unseen, and aspects of the divine. Marion links the invisible to the act of painting, specifically, through the notion of the unseen. As a painting develops, the painter operates with an intuitive logic of choices that wrest entirely unforeseen and original new forms from the realm of the unseen.

The problem is that this represents one aspect of the psychology of artistic creation as though it were a sufficient account of the ontology of art, which it is not. True, the painter mainly creates texture and detail in a work by applying brushstrokes in a way that cannot be predicted exactly. But there are many great painters who have created a great painting simply by realizing a composition worked out in previous studies; structural features of the work, in other words, may well involve a translation from work already seen in another dimension of the visible.

It should also be emphasized that Marion's claim of absolute originality holds no water when it comes to the work that ends up on the canvas, whatever the psychology of its origins. He announces peremptorily that the painter's originality is "without exemplar, model, or precedent."[35] In terms of originality, however, the decisive criterion is how a work appears to sight in comparison with the appearance of other works by the artist, as well as works by other artists. In psychological terms, the choices one makes in doing a painting—even one that seeks to copy another exactly—are unpredictable. We know what the work must end up being like, but how the image is realized in terms of choice of brushstrokes is relatively open. And if the artist is not copying another work, then this openness is even more the case. Indeed, abstract art or a child's splashing around with paint is radicalized even further with respect to originality construed on this basis. But there is nothing "authentic" about all this in itself; the unpredictability of placing marks—its intuitive logic—is not a criterion of originality at all but simply what is involved in making a painting as such.

Marion's emphasis on the absoluteness of originality in authentic painting is likewise not viable. When the painter negotiates his or her canvas, the marks that are applied are not simply developed as intuitive choices in relation to the accumulating whole, but equally through a sense of what is appropriate in the light of the artist's previous work and experience of works by other artists. Of course, in terms of psychological intentions these references are "unseen," in the sense that one cannot "see" what is going on in the artist's mind as he or she makes choices. But as was noted earlier, this is irrelevant, for what determines the originality of such choices is not their intuitive psychology but how they compare with works already achieved by the artist and, more fundamentally, by others.

What a choice amounts to in terms of originality is only meaningful in a horizon of critical comparisons. An artist such as Turner, for example, is original in a far deeper sense than any of his British contemporaries because his innovations involve new approaches to fundamentals of the medium, based on light and form; he explores these to extremes achieved by no other artist of that time. In turn, this originality allows other artists to learn from it; it becomes exemplary.

For an artist's work to become exemplary means that other artists learn from it explicitly. In some cases this may amount to little more than copying, but with the best artists it becomes an influence that is absorbed, adapted to the painter's individual style, and then developed into something new. Marion's account, however, fails to take any account of such criteria of originality. For him, the painter's choices have no exemplars or models; they are in effect ineffable emanations of genius. And all that he offers in justification of this extreme claim is repetition—based on ever more exaggerated hyperbole—rather than compelling argument. The following is an example:

> Like the surface of the earth, which is fractured and folded under the pressure
> of the invisible earthly forces, the magma of the unseen seeps out from the folds
> that, from the inside, take shape in the frame of the painting, rising to its surface
> like the fossils deposited by a torrent of lava. The painter by his sensitive hand
> and quasi-vulcanology, follows with a flowing brush . . . the radically unforeseen
> trait that imposes itself.[36]

This—and Marion's many other quasi-mystical effusions in the same vein—explains nothing about originality in painting but only leads to the aforementioned psychological irrelevances.

The problem, then, is that while Marion's emphasis on originality is, in effect, the basis of a distinction between mere painting and artistic painting, he does not handle it at all convincingly. This is because his basic approach—in terms of both strategy and outcomes—is driven by the authority of theology, as manifested in the fact that his key operative concept is not painting as art but rather authentic painting. And this authenticity is grounded in the invisible.

We will recall that the invisible incorporates perspective, the gaze, the unseen, and the divine. Perspective provides a necessary orientation to the gaze, but Marion gradually increases his emphasis on the invisible subjective intentions and feelings that are its substance. He searches for an idiom of painting where, instead of the invisible being lost or arrested in the denuded visibilia of minimalism or the spectacular emptiness of the mere image, the visible will actually diminish itself so to affirm the invisible. It will lead us to a crossing of gazes—to real communication rather than to private sensory pleasure.

This is why he places such emphasis on the icon. As explained earlier, the painted gaze of the religious figure is one that suppresses its own visibility to join our gaze with an evocation of that of the prototype; thus the visible gives way to a complex affirmation of the invisible. In this regard, Marion emphasizes that the icon embodies a relation exemplified by Christ himself: Christ lived, acted, and died so as to suppress his own being as a visible corporeal person and thereby to direct our gaze to the supreme invisible, namely, God himself.

Now, while Marion is clearly privileging "icon" in its customary usage—as a synonym for "devotional object"—he does suggest that other formats in the history of art as well have likewise achieved authentic painting. According to him, the authentic function of the image is as follows:

> Not a single image claims self-sufficiency, but rather returns itself to an Other—this can be accomplished in a number of ways: either by digging the visible screen from a counter-gaze found to be invisible (as in "the icons," Roman and Gothic sculpture); or by diverting light outside of its function of illuminating the present toward the summons of the Infinite, of the invisible, of the unattainable (as in Baroque domes, Rubens, etc.); or by employing shadows and lights not to confirm the visible shapes but rather to confound and disrupt for the sake of the undecidable appearance of the invisible Spirit (Caravaggio, Rembrandt, Nain).[37]

What all these have in common is that "the prestige of the image or the visible object impoverishes itself, imposing limits on itself so that the veneration is brought back not to itself, the image, but rather to the prototype, possibly aimed at through it."[38]

In the foregoing remarks, Marion identifies specific painterly features that are conducive to evoking the religious invisible, including the suggestion of the infinite through nonnaturalistic light effects and the suggestion of the indeterminable appearance of spirit through chiaroscuro (though he does not note the relevant technical term), based on dramatic contrasts of light and shadow. But while he links these to the prototype, he does not even begin to explain the character of the link. There are, indeed, many works of visual art that suggest the infinite or the unattainable, or whatever; many of Caspar David Friedrich's landscapes, for example, have been taken to be significant in exactly this regard.[39] But the suggestion of the infinite is one thing; the interpretation of it in religious terms is another. Infinity is not ipso facto a religiously significant concept: interpreted literally, it is no more than an ontological or metaphysical factor that is psychologically overwhelming if one tries to imagine what it amounts to. For it to have religious meaning over and above this surely presupposes some active mediating element that allows it to be so understood. The prototype, in other words, is not religiously meaningful in itself.

Similar considerations are pertinent to the other examples mentioned by Marion, namely, the art of the baroque and the effects of chiaroscuro. In ordinary life, we often encounter illuminated forms and plays of shadow that may suggest that matter is subtended (or even sustained) by a phenomenally indeterminable realm of spirit. Such a suggestion, however, is likely to be fleeting and to amount to no more than a vague sense of the mystical: that there is more to things than meets the eye.

These elaborations point toward the weaknesses of Marion's position. In painting, mystical allusions may endure for as long as the painting survives; being fixed, however, they lack the physical transience that evokes the mystical as experienced in the world of immediate perception. Accordingly, in order to talk of such experience in the context of painting we must explain how painting intervenes upon the prototype and energizes its religious significance. Yet Marion offers no account of what this intervention might amount to. Without it, we have "prototypes" but without the intrinsic religious meaning he wishes to assign to them.

And this is the problem. Marion implies that the prototype is a feature of the icon of religious painting—exclusively. But it is not, as the examples of Friedrich and of baroque art just mentioned demonstrate; we have prototypes that are not of intrinsic religious significance. Indeed, it can be argued that any picture of anything (from the prephotographic age) that is no longer extant involves a prototype: because it has gone into the past, there is nothing for us to compare it with to determine the picture's accuracy. It is clear that things must be taken beyond Marion's standpoint.

In order to do so, it must first be emphasized that the visible features of a painting evoke imaginative possibilities of experience that may involve identifications with the artist's vision per se or the way in which this particular subject matter is presented. The latter case involves a sense of the active relation between what is in the work and the represented content to which it refers; here there is a role for the "prototype" as the subject matter that the artist interprets, and changes the appearance of, through the activity of drawing or painting.

The visibility of the finished painting evokes the temporal coming-to-be of those gestures and mark placings whereby its finished visibility is enabled. Our gaze crosses an invisible prototype of the artist's gaze and gestural activity through our imagining of how it might have worked in the very process of creation itself. This realm of the prototype as activity can encompass other factors as well. What is visible in the completed painting may provoke imaginings as to how this subject matter (in figurative art, at least) came to be encountered by the artist, and/or what its existence might have been like independent of the artist's treatment of it, or indeed, whether it actually existed at all.

This is not simply an art historical question about sources; it is an imaginative crossing of our gaze into the secret of the artist's original encounter with or formulation of the represented item or states of affairs. Is the finished painting a visual completion of aesthetic possibilities presented by the original, or was the original even richer in such possibilities? Or did the prototype involve the painter's merely painting something from memory or from imagination?

In fact, even if we are actually present when something is painted, we have a complex role in this encounter with the prototype. Our watching the process of creation is not some passively registered sequence of sense-impressions. The meaning of the process is ambiguous even as it happens, inasmuch as it is comprehensible under different aspects. But which of these are the decisive aspects? We see the artist put certain marks on a surface, but the question of what is actually going on in this act of interpretation is itself an act of interpretation on our part—and this is true to some extent even if the painter actually verbalizes what he or she is doing. These ambiguities, moreover, are amplified when the event of creation has gone into the past. The picture's visible content points to its origins in the painter's prototypical acting on the subject and provokes different avenues of imaginative projection in terms of how this might have happened.

Thus we see that if a painting is art and not mere painting, what is visible in the work exists so as to engage all the complex invisible factors just described. The perspectival content of a painting does not—as Marion suggests—have to make the invisible do service on behalf of the visible; rather, it can bring the two into a mutually enhancing reciprocity. It is important to emphasize the notion of "reciprocity" here, which suggests that the crossing of the viewer's and the artist's gaze expresses the fact that these are ultimately dependent on one another. Mutual respect is the logical consequence of this. Marion's account of the icon's prototype, in contrast, is authoritarian. For him, the visibility of the icon is meant to be self-suppressing so as to evoke the original gaze of the prototype. This is not an open and exploring gaze but one that demands submission to the greater religious truth that it is conveying. Whatever mutuality is involved in the crossing of gazes here is a limited one; it amounts to no more than a sharing governed by strict doctrinal boundaries.

Such an approach is also highly reductive. The meaning that Marion assigns to the icon applies just as well to cheap copies and even to kitschy plaster saints and crucifixes and the like. In terms of his theory, it would follow that these are even more authentic than artistic items, for in them it is the very banality of how they are made that facilitates the overlooking of their particular visible character in favor of the prototypic gaze of the saint or whoever it is that this character points toward.

### Conclusion

We have seen that Marion's theory of the icon is profoundly problematic. He suggests, in passing, that the strategy of the icon is "aesthetic,"[40] but he offers not the slightest criterion whereby the icon's meaning can be taken to be anything other than a religious message. He leaves us at the level of vulgar piety—an assessment made all the more compelling by his bald assertion that "the liturgy alone impoverishes the image enough to wrest it from every spectacle."[41]

Things need not be left at the level of vulgar piety, however. In this regard, it is useful to note that in effect Marion commits the same kind of mistake as those who demand that authentic painting have a politically correct content. Yet as Walter Benjamin saw (in one of his rare moments of genuine insight), political art is only authentically art when its political significance flows from the innovative artistic character of the work rather than from overtly political content.[42] This is an important clue: perhaps we can find some religious meaning implicit in the specific kind of originality achieved by artists rather than in the prototypic gaze of religious figures.

Teasing this out will take us far beyond Marion. He rightly senses a connection between picturing and a priori factors in experience but fails to ground this connection adequately. And while he is right to look for religious significance in the nature of perspective and the role of the infinite, we must look elsewhere for its grounding. In the final chapter, accordingly, I shall outline an alternative metaphysics and theology of pictorial art.

# 7 METAPHYSICS AND THEOLOGY OF PICTORIAL ART

## Introduction

Throughout this book, I have argued that pictorial art intervenes upon and transforms that which it represents. The religious significance of the metaphysical aspect of pictorial art is the subject of this final chapter. Such an emphasis is unusual: pictorial art and religious meaning are usually studied in terms of identifying which religious figures a work represents and the way in which they are represented. Marion offers a partial contemporary alternative to this, but as we have seen, his position is riven by difficulties.

Yet he at least points us in a useful direction, toward identifying metaphysical structures in pictorial art that are of religious significance. My approach will go further, arguing that the very making of pictorial art involves metaphysical factors that can also be interpreted as disclosing aspects of humanity's relation to the Godhead. Such religious meaning, however, emerges only when the metaphysical evidence has been established on independent philosophical grounds and is then reconsidered in the context of faith. Some examples of this have already been discussed in earlier chapters; the present chapter will take the approach much further, albeit in somewhat speculative terms.

### I

To begin, let us consider the universe without reference to the existence of self-conscious life. In its strictly physical being, the universe exists only as matter in a constant state of change. Its past states have gone and its future states do not yet exist. Without some dimension wherein its previous states and possible states are projected, there are no grounds on which its actuality can comprise anything other than changing matter per se. Time exists as a process but not as past or future or as alternative possibilities of process. Indeed, one cannot even describe matter in process as occupying a "present."

The notion of a present makes sense only in relation to an observer. "Present" can, of course, be used as a mere synonym for a hypothetical determinate position in space-time; it provides a notional point in relation to which we might talk of present, past, and future. But a point marked out on a continuum is not a present, unless its relation to the past and the future actively shape it. For the present to be real—in ontological rather than merely notional or methodological terms—it must involve an observer who actively experiences it in the context of past and future, that is to say, a self-conscious being with powers of memory, imagination, and symbolization. Through these powers the universe is qualitatively changed. Self-consciousness is, in effect, an intervention on the physical; it introduces present, past, future, and possibility into the physical world. This means that the character of space is changed, for as we saw earlier, if something did not occupy some portion of space—however miniscule—there would be no grounds for saying that it existed at all. Space occupancy seems the most basic criterion for saying that something has being. Even sounds, albeit invisible, are perturbations of the atmosphere that impact upon the eardrums and thus occupy space.

Now, in a universe without observers there are surely extended spatial masses in a process of change. Such spatial masses are heterogeneous—they must differ from one another, otherwise change would not be possible. These differences pertain to intrinsic physical properties, as well as such features as scale, size, shape, density, volume, and the like. But these features do not exist "neat," as it were; a fly negotiates the same spatial masses as a human, but for the former, the character of their extension is very different than it is for the latter.

The foregoing may be illustrated by the distinction between the macroscopic and microscopic properties of spatial extension, which are distinguished on the basis of what is and what is not accessible to immediate perceptual inspection. But if we exclude reference to perception, then there are no grounds for making a distinction between the macroscopic and microscopic.[1] As noted just above, spatial extension conceived of in the absence of an observer becomes entirely abstract; for something to be spatially extended in any determinate sense, the character of its extension must be correlated with how it can tracked and mapped by the cognitive activity of an observer.

In this, the human observer has a singular advantage over the fly or any other sentient life-form, for that matter. The temporal horizon allows spatial extension not only to be made determinate but to be acted upon. Space is thus made meaningful. This is not just a case of its being endowed with a narrative structure; it also means that past, anticipated future, and projected possible configurations of space now inform the universe's processes through the things that human beings think and do. The universe becomes a world.

Let us focus on the key contrast here. What happens in a purely physical universe is the outcome of a strictly linear causal succession of previous states. Past states, being no longer existent, cannot come back to occasion new physical changes; and future states, not yet having existed, cannot bring about physical changes in what precedes them. But the self-conscious agent's ideas of present, past, and future, as well as possibility, are ideas upon which such an agent can act and bring about changes in the physical universe. This network of ideas enables agency that can break with strictly linear causal physical succession and thus constitute the basis of a new, emergent level of being. As factors in such agency, present, past, and future have real existence as a temporal horizon wherein the brute physical process is made meaningful.

Anything a self-conscious agent does or makes exemplifies—in both its execution and outcomes—an understanding of the temporal horizon, which in this way is given physical expression. As well as being integral to all thought and action, however, past, present, future, and possibility admit of representation through visual imagination and memory, that is, those modes of mental projection with a quasi-sensory visual character. For present purposes, let us call this "iconic projection."

This does not just involve mental activity. The images produced by iconic projection have elements of consistency with how their objects appeared or might appear as extended in space. Hence, while an image of something does not cause its object to exist, it nevertheless, as an iconic image, embodies some aspect of its object's spatially extended character or of the way in which its object might be extended. Iconic projection works by means of doubling space, as it were, through engaging with both the past and the realm of possibility. Through visual imagination and memory, space is projected in virtual terms, allowing the immediate spatial aspects of things to be made intelligible in relation to other spatial aspects—past, future, and possible. Iconic projection, in other words, articulates space across the horizon of time. It can thus be de-scribed as "space-worlding"—the means whereby space and its occupants come to exist in a fuller or more complete sense.

This passage to completion has one more, higher stage, embodied when iconic projection is realized through a physical medium such as pictorial rep-resentation rather than through mental activity alone. Let us now address this.

## II

Pictures represent through having some spatially extended features of visual appearance in common with that which they are representations of. (Texts, in contrast, do not have to look like what they are talking about.) Every picture is, by definition, "of" a three-dimensional subject projected in a virtually two-dimensional medium. In this regard, it should be noted that there are no two-dimensional entities in an absolute physical sense. Two-dimensionality is an ideal state. Flat physical surfaces can approximate it but never embody it completely.

In the case of picturing, we are dealing with an ideal planar structure lim-ited by the edges of the picture. This basic structure is constituted by a fore-ground plane, where the represented pictorial space is closest to the viewer, and a background plane, which is furthest from the viewer; this planar struc-ture is, logically speaking, the central feature of pictorial representation. All that is necessary for something to be a picture is that it have a virtual three-dimensional content of a recognizable kind occupying the space between the foreground and background planes. Even the most basic painting presents a possible state of visual affairs or (in the case of "paradoxical" artists like M. C. Escher) a combination of such possibilities.

In those cases where a painting takes as its subject something that has actu-ally existed (as in portraits, still lifes, and landscapes, for example), it allows aspects of the being of something that once existed to have continuing effects in the present of its current reception and the interpretations involved in such reception. It should be emphasized, however, that the use of picturing to denote some item or state of affairs that exists or did exist is just one of its uses; it can be an intention that guides the making of a picture, but it is not necessary in order to make a picture as such.

Let us suppose, then, that one has learned to how to make a picture using pictorial space in the sense just described. One might think this is no more than a useful skill, but it is far more than that. As we have seen throughout this book, through iconic projection humans can create simulacra of times and places that they do not presently occupy or create projections of things, places, and times that are not part of the actual order of events—fantasy worlds and impossible scenarios. Through making a picture we generate spatial extension in virtual as well as real terms. Such creation has the character of modal plasticity. Through learning how spatial extension appears, we can imaginatively twist it and bend it, thus making reality itself, in symbolic terms, subject to the will.

This is the supreme idealization of possibility itself. One can, of course, entertain possibilities by merely thinking about them or writing them into poems or stories. But picturing, in contrast, presents possibility at the same ontological level as the very criterion of something's existing—namely, spatial extension. The picture is made of real physical material that the artist configures so as to project a virtual content. And in this it has a kind of intrinsic enigmatic quality. Being finite, it will eventually be destroyed one way or another in the passage of time, but its virtual content as virtual is not implicated in this destruction. The content lives in its material base and is tied to the destiny of that base, but it does not itself change and decay; it is possibility idealized.

There is another enigmatic level involved that has been touched on throughout this book. To understand an event in time one must follow the pattern of its unfolding in linear terms: the elements in the event must be comprehended in the exact order of their occurrence or else we will be unable to make any sense of them. The unity of a spatially extended object, in contrast, does not require such linear apprehension of its parts; one can get a sense of its identity as both individual and kind by exploring its parts in any order. One view of it may be enough; alternatively, one might want to look at all sides of it. But logically we are not constrained to explore these sides in any specific order; the spatial object has an open unity.

The picture has this character by virtue of being a physically extended object, but it has this character at a second level as well, that of the represented subject matter given in pictorial space. We can recognize the subject and its recessional setting by moving from the distance to the foreground or vice versa or from left to right or right to left; the direction of exploration is not logically tied to any specific direction. The pictorial content as well as its physical base has an open unity.

The importance of this consists in its relation to the temporal horizon, which, as suggested previously, is internalized in pictorial space as the context for presentness. The past, present, and future as such have their own logical relation—an order in which they necessarily must occur; but here we are em-

phasizing their horizonal character. How humans understand temporal concepts is open. We can act in the present making direct reference to the past
or future: we can do things in the present trying to rectify past errors; we can
negotiate time on the basis of hunches about what might be possible. The flow
of time cannot be controlled by will, but how we inhabit it can be, to greater or
lesser degrees.

Again, it is important to emphasize that pictorial art achieves all this
through its particular mode of being visible. It works both through occupying
space and through representing a pictorial or optical space populated by virtual three-dimensional entities that are isomorphic with the spatially extended
possible states of affairs that the work represents. Hence, inasmuch as the criterion of something's physically existing is its occupation of a determinate area
of space-time, it follows that pictorial art not only expresses the temporal horizon but is, literally, its physical concretion. Such art involves the creation of
a real physical object the perception of whose virtual space involves an opening up of the temporal horizon through spatial properties. The space-worlding
of iconic projection is realized as a physical feature *in* the spatially extended
world. The temporal horizon becomes congruent with itself; it achieves a kind
of completion.

It might be asked how sculpture relates to these points. The creation of
sculpture involves the creation of individual forms whose relation to a broader
systematic background of other visible things tends to be suppressed. In the
case of sculptural friezes, something of this broader network of connections
begins to emerge—but only because it here begins to approximate the idiom of
illusion that characterizes pictorial art.

Now let us turn to that which is at the heart of freedom and autonomy in
pictorial art, namely, the creative individual who makes the work. The finished
drawing or painting is an organic whole in the most complete terms. Again, as
has been stressed throughout this book, all the individually contingent moments
of deliberation and gesture that were involved in making the painting are transformed into necessity once the work is completed. This necessity is made perceptible inasmuch as the work's final appearance is as it is only because of the exact
sequence of deliberation and activity that went into its making. In nonartistic
painting, these factors are overlooked in favor of the informational function that
the image serves. But in artistic painting we attend to the work as a completed
whole whose achieved identity is logically inseparable from those individually
contingent and temporally spread-out gestures involved in its making.

If this approach is correct, then painting has an extraordinary metaphysical significance whose structure has scarcely been touched upon by the existing literature. It is not only a physical concretion of the temporal horizon, but it is also one that presents—in immediate spatial terms—individually contingent moments of experience transformed into necessity. All the gestures and brush-strokes that went into its making could have been done otherwise, but when the work is complete they are now inseparable from its final appearance. *This* particular finished work embodies exactly *that* process of creation.

At the heart of this engagement is the distinctiveness of the artist's style. And this discloses a further truth: the temporal horizon does not evolve as a dry formula but as something emergent from entities who, as space-occupying bodies, have a unique perspective upon the universe. Individual members of a species share the same basic cognitive capacities, but these capacities are conceptually connected to individuality. For example, in a normal, healthy person memory and imagination recollect or project (respectively) past or possible perceptual scenarios from the viewpoint of an individual person in an individual body. It is nature, of course, that creates the individual through configurations of matter and physical laws, but the individual transcends these origins. This is disclosed in a heightened way through pictorial art. When original, such art shows that the artist has been able to go beyond the stylistic routines and norms of the medium. Such going-beyond is a natural gift—it cannot be achieved by simply following rules. But this gift is the opposite of mere natural mechanism, for it is reciprocally connected with how the subject's self-consciousness is developed through practical expression. Nature creates the individual through its physical laws, but the individual in turn adapts natural materials or stuffs manufactured from it in ways that embody and enhance self-understanding.

Pictorial art shows this to the highest degree. In it the reciprocity of the temporal horizon and the individual self-conscious being, together with the reciprocity of nature and creative individuality, are made visible at the level of physical space-occupancy itself. Originality of style awakens interest in how the painting aesthetically opens up specific aspects of the temporal horizon and how the character of this opening clarifies the scope of the individual style through which the opening is achieved. Pictorial art shows something about what we are. And what it shows is something that exceeds any survival-oriented instinct, even if it is, in phylogenetic terms, emergent from it. A self-conscious being is one whose being, irrespective of what the agent believes or intends, has a broader ontological role vis-à-vis the universe. The agent's mode of being tends to complete being, and painting does this at the level of space-occupancy.

It should be emphasized that it is one thing to have an ordered universe but another thing entirely for its order to be completed through the reciprocity of the temporal horizon and the individual agent's perspective on it. This latter development and its embodiment in pictorial art is so extraordinary as to suggest that the metaphysical meaning just described is indicative of a broader destiny. This may be shown by a religious interpretation of painting's metaphysical significance. Occam's razor, of course, would suggest that no further interpretation is required. But in fact there is quite a bit more that can be said, centering on whether we have the faith to interpret painting's metaphysical meaning in religious terms as well.

## III

This issue can be approached, initially, through a few thoughts on the nature of God. If one is a believer, then God, the Supreme Being, is regarded as the maker of worlds and the ground and sustainer of the entire universe. God is a self-sufficient, self-determining entity who creates and comprehends all space and time in absolute terms. In creating space and the possibility of human evolution, God introduces the temporal horizon into the universe and gives it completion through the emergence of self-conscious beings with free agency. In their self-consciousness and free agency, such beings exist in the image of God.

Ironically, however, if such beings are to achieve true autonomy and self-consciousness, then God cannot be an explicit player in this development. Suppose, for example, that the Supreme Being is taken to create matter and then order it into a world complete with a holy text explaining why humanity was created, with reward-and-punishment-based rules for obeying and loving divine strictures, and so on. This artisanal idea of God would actually reduce the principle of divine creativity to a model derived from the finite world, namely, that of the benevolent despot. But if a Supreme Being is self-creating and self-determining, it follows that beings made in the divine image must have finite equivalents of these features as defining characteristics. As finite, they must be creatures who have evolved into self-consciousness and autonomy. And if this self-consciousness and autonomy exemplifies the image of God, it must be explored for its own sake, that is, for self-exploration and accomplishment rather than the augmentation of instinct- and survival-oriented activity. Beings of this sort must *find* their way back to God through reflection upon their freedom and its implications rather than by simply following the supposed instructions arising from the literal interpretation of holy texts. Beings made in God's image require autonomy, not authority, in order to recognize the ultimate ground of their existence.

This has complex implications. For if God really is the Supreme Being, then divine artifice cannot be seen to directly sustain the meaning of what self-conscious beings do, even though God creates and sustains the fabric that allows them to make things meaningful. For those created in God's own image, the return to God must be a rational inquiry that reaches a point where—in order to recognize God in our own nature—we must take a leap of faith based on independently established metaphysical truths rather than theological authority or revelation alone. In other words, God's being must be shown rather than said in what is created, but this showing must also allow for an overt saying based on the faith-directed interpretation of independently established truths.

In the preceding sections relevant metaphysical arguments that hold without the involvement of any religious standpoint have been put forward. Now the time has come to take a leap of faith, in order to see if these truths might allow for a further—religious—interpretation. In the context of pictorial art, this can be done as follows. As we have seen, through the intervention of self-consciousness the physical universe is not only made meaningful but also, in a sense, brought to a higher and more complete state of being. Through the activity and artifice of self-conscious individuals, the otherwise nonexistent space of present, past, future, and possibility actively shapes the existence of the physical universe in the form of a temporal horizon. And in pictorial art the drama of this intervention and completion is expressed in a way that physically embodies aspects of the horizon at the ontologically fundamental level of space-occupancy itself. It is this that gives such art a metaphysically privileged status.

The religious significance of this can be expressed in the first instance through some general points. For example, since God creates the beings that embody the temporal horizon and express it spatially, one can conclude that, through this, God's purpose is immanent to the physical world. If this is so, then it follows that pictorial art's spatialization of the temporal horizon is not only a making-meaningful of the universe but also an expression of divine purpose. There is more to it than that, however. As shown earlier, pictorial art is the physical concretion of this at the decisive level of space-occupancy. When a work issues in an artwork rather than mere visual information, it can be interpreted as a mode of image-making that is itself an image of God's being as the opener of time.

This opening has further significance. God's essence must be to create—there seems to be no alternative to this. Now, since the physical universe as we perceive it is subject to the laws of nature, it has mechanistic necessity. Some proponents of quantum theory might deny that this is true at the microlevel, but at the macrolevel lawfulness unquestionably holds. The question arises, then, as to whether the divine essence is constrained by the lawfulness of nature and the rationality of creation. Of course, if God is all-powerful, then the divine essence is the creator of what appears to us as necessary. But if God is rational, then it follows that what is divinely created must not be free in an arbitrary sense; it must be done for a reason. And if it is done for a reason, then it follows that the realization of that end requires a specific means that is not just a case of what the creator wants. God must follow rules.

Freedom in human artifice, of course, is a matter of how one follows rules that govern the kind of artifice in question. However, if God really is all-powerful, then divine rule-following must somehow involve artifice wherein the elements of necessity and freedom in making are inseparable; for God, rule-following and freedom must be as one. This is hard to make sense of, from any finite analytic viewpoint; however, the creation of pictorial art offers at least symbolic exemplification of it. Every stroke and gesture in the accumulating whole of the work has an element of contingency in it: though guided by the developing whole, the artist can still pick and choose how the development should be continued. But, as we saw earlier, when the work is complete, its identity as this particular work is dependent on the exact brushstrokes (or whatever) that were accumulated gradually so to create the finished work. This essence of the final product entails, as it were, the existence of this exact passage of bringing-forth. There is a harmony of freedom and necessity that is based on the artist's free choice in developing and completing the composition

Although this might be said of artworks in any medium, pictorial art has an extra dimension of relevant meaning. Whereas the unity of the literary or musical work involves a linear temporal structure, that of the picture is not constrained in this way. The open unity of the pictorial artwork as a spatial object means that the holistic necessity described above operates with an extra dimension of freedom: while the scanning of such unity is a temporal process, it does not have to follow a rigidly linear order in terms of which parts are scanned.

Likewise, as explained earlier, the picture not only has open unity by virtue of being a physical, space-occupying object but also has it at the level of its emergent virtual three-dimensional features. We can recognize the picture's subject matter and recessional setting by moving from the distance to the foreground or vice versa or from left to right or vice versa. The direction of exploration is not logically tied to any specific direction; the pictorial content as well as its physical planar base has an open unity.

Now, one assumes that in creating the world of spatio-temporal things, God does not follow a simple linear temporal process of creation. This would reduce divine creativity to the model of human artifice. Indeed, if what God created continued to exist without further divine involvement, it would mean that such things were now, in effect, limits to that existence. It is more logical to assume that God creates things, giving them form and being, but that the form and being in question are constantly sustained by divine will. The universe is not the outcome of a linear process, however much it appears that way from a finite perspective. We should see it, rather, as emergent from the divine essence.

The twofold open unity of pictorial art's meaning is a symbol of this emergence. The three-dimensional narrative features are given their character by their dependence on the physical material of the picture, but how they emerge from this is not tied to a simple linear progression. There are alternative vectors and emphases in how we perceptually explore the emergence of virtual content from the planar base. The being of the picture is not that of something that was simply brought into existence. We recognize, rather, that it is something whose essence is expressed through being constantly perceptible under different aspects. Tracing the emergence of this three-dimensional meaning from the planar base is a dynamic and inexhaustible activity. In other words, the open character of emergent meaning in the pictorial artwork gives its created ontology a symbolic kinship with God's creation and sustaining of the universe.

This open unity has further significance. When an individual is known to God, it is through the totality of events in the narrative of his or her life rather than the narrative that is completed at the point of death. Obviously the end stage has a special significance, but it is not just in terms of that end stage that God comprehends us. In the work of pictorial art, the work is finished; we recognize it as a picture of such and such a thing or state of affairs. But its open unity means that we can see the end product and the aspects through which the narrative is enabled in direct relation to one another. Indeed, to aesthetically appreciate the pictorial work is to take account of this relation as well as the material (considered in the broadest ontological terms) from which the work is constituted. In pictorial art, all the relevant factors are presented simultaneously. Again, of course, through being finite, the human subject cannot comprehend them all simultaneously, but the work itself makes them available in such terms. It is an image of God's total comprehension of all the aspects of something's existence.

The role of virtual three-dimensionality in pictorial ontology has further religious significance. God's essence is not constrained by spatio-temporal factors; indeed, it is the divine essence that sustains them. But while we can understand this essence in crude terms, it cannot be understood sufficiently. God's creative intelligence sustains our world but is of a different ontological order.

Now, as well as the picture's open unity having a significance in this respect, so does its planar structure. Under one aspect, of course, the picture is just a flat material surface "in" which we see three-dimensional structures. However, the logical basis of this referential function does not depend on a physically flat surface; if an artist is clever enough, even a physical surface with lumps and grooves can conceal these physical features and simply appear as a plane from which a virtual three-dimensional space is projected. That is to say, there are no absolutely two-dimensional surfaces; they have ideal existence only. The basis of pictorial representation in logical terms is based on the relation between virtual three-dimensionality and notional two-dimensionality. This means that the mutually dependent worlds of the work's material reality and its virtual content are themselves sustained by a different ontological realm—the ideal two-dimensional plane. The emergence of pictorial meaning, like that of the spatio-temporal world, is dependent on an essence that manifests itself materially but that cannot be understood sufficiently in material terms. Again we find kinship between pictorial art and the divine.

This kinship extends to the content of pictorial art as well. This does not refer to picturing's capacity to represent religiously meaningful subject matter but rather to its capacity to transform how reality appears. The phenomenon of modal plasticity has already been mentioned. Pictorial art is about striving to actualize the possible through wishing and making; the artist makes the picture, but what or she makes has a virtual content encompassing represented things and states and affairs that are emergent from the work's material base. What is thus created is only a possible appearance, but it is at least a crude image of God's ectypal intelligence wherein being can be created through thinking of or intending it. Literature and music have this aspect as well. But the vital point about pictorial art is that this image of the ectypal is realized at the highest level of existence itself, namely, space-occupancy. Literature and music can be embodied in space-occupying texts and scores, but this space-occupancy is not a part of their meaning as literature and music.

While pictorial art has a special role in relation to the image of divine consciousness, this does not rule out the other art media having their own special relation to this. Indeed, there are a few features shared by all the arts that can be related to their status as images of divine consciousness. For example, God's creation or sustaining of the universe does not involve constant revisions so as to get it right; once created, the universe follows its course. The work of art can be revised at any time the creator pleases, but mostly, once it has been created, the artist will leave it as it is. The artist's relation to the work, in other words, is akin to God's relation to the universe; in principle, the work could be added to, but if the decision is made that it is complete, then it is complete.

There is an additional relevant factor. It is often noted how artistic meaning involves an element of ineffability. Yet our day-to-day language is not like this; we communicate facts, descriptions, beliefs, and the like and expect that these will be recognized and acted upon without undue deliberation as to the nuances of their meaning. The meaning of an artwork, in contrast, cannot be reduced to such simple recognition. We can describe its structure in literal terms, but the meaning that is emergent from this cannot be sufficiently paraphrased. We know what the picture or novel or whatever represents, but its complete meaning exceeds what can be put into words. Indeed, the very idea of an artwork having a complete meaning is not altogether intelligible. Whatever the finished work is, it becomes physically discontinuous from the creator as soon as it is completed. Thereafter, the artist him- or herself changes and cannot recover the original process of creation in exact terms or erase intervening experiences so as to "return" to the work exactly at the point it was left. Indeed, even at the point of leaving, the artist knows that what he or she becomes in the future will invest the work with a different meaning and that all those who come to the work after its completion will engage with it from their own existential viewpoints. The artist, in other words, offers a possibility of visual experience whose very essence is to be developed further—to have its meaning revised just as the circumstances of how it is perceived and received change.

There is, of course, a simple logical explanation for this. The artwork is a unique individual or type encountered as a sensible or imaginatively intended object; in order to comprehend it, we must have direct experience of it.

Inasmuch as aesthetic meaning inheres in this fabric of particularity, it cannot be paraphrased, because literal description through language is of a different ontological order. As soon as description tries to project the appearance of a sensible or imaginatively intended item that we have not directly perceived or imaginatively intended at some point, it uses terms that are inherently ambiguous. We all may know what the phrase "an intensely scarlet velvet robe" means, but there are countless shades of intensely velvet scarlet and varieties of robe, as well as countless different ways that these may be conjectured by the individual. When it comes to further judgments—such as whether this shade of scarlet and this weave of velvet involve an aesthetically satisfying relation—matters become even more dependent on direct perceptual acquaintance with the aesthetic object.

Recent work in aesthetics has not engaged with this factor adequately.[2] There has been much debate about the scope of "aesthetic testimony": the possibility of forming aesthetic beliefs without direct acquaintance. What is remarkable, however, is how the discussion has been pitched mainly at the level of talk about aesthetic properties and artworks rather than an investigation of the perceptual basis of our recognition of art as art. In fact, many of these discussions never even discuss any artworks in a sustained way or offer any criterion of the aesthetic at all. One development is particularly bizarre, namely, the tendency to describe the view that aesthetic beliefs cannot be derived from testimony as a "pessimistic" standpoint.[3] In a sense, the exact opposite is the case: the very fact that aesthetic judgment cannot be based on secondhand reports alone affirms the nonreductive, ontologically autonomous character of the aesthetic, that is, the fact that it is a distinctive phenomenon that cannot be reduced to mere description. It is the possibility of aesthetic testimony that is really the pessimistic viewpoint.

This viewpoint, indeed, distorts another positive feature. The ontological divide between description or paraphrase and the fullness of artistic meaning is actually a key player in our aesthetic appreciation. Our enjoyment of the work cannot find sufficient words to describe the meaning, yet it would like to. There is a striving to make our understanding adequate to the richer meaning. If this were just a case of bridging the divide between sensuous/imaginative meaning and abstract language as an intellectual exercise, it might be of little interest. But the ontological divide in question both separates and relates us to the being of something, namely, the artwork as a unity created to engage with an audience. To engage with the work is to search for a meaning that comprises both the sensuous / imaginatively intended particular and the personal vision embodied in it, a meaning that can never be fully comprehended. Our striving knows this, yet knows also that—through our very striving to understand—we will find some clarification of our own existential issues and aesthetic empathy with the artistic vision embodied in the work.

Here, in other words, the ineffability of artistic meaning is a focus for self-understanding. And in this respect it is akin to the believer's relation to God. For the religious believer, God is manifest in the sensible world. The divine presence is recognizable through the incomplete character of the universe considered as an infinitely divisible series of entities in relation with one another. Something complete must sustain all this. We talk of divine omnipotence, omniscience, love, and the like, but in the final analysis, these properties are terms that do not even begin to evoke God's power of ontological completion. God is ineffable. Nevertheless, for the believer the very physicality of the physical universe demands that we make sense of what completes it. And even though we cannot comprehend this completion except as a bare idea, we can at least engage with its immeasurable ontological fullness. This engagement both questions and finds us a place in the scheme of things.

Of course, the enjoyment of artistic meaning is not based on religious grounds as such. But the point is that the ineffability of artistic meaning is symbolic of the religious domain. It is an aspect of a rational sensibility that searches for self-understanding through striving toward a meaning that is known to be ineffable and unattainable. Just as God's presence in nature draws us toward it, no matter how ineffable, so too the artist's creative vision in the artwork draws us to a higher meaning. The latter is a crude image of the former.

There is a final corollary to this. No human being can see the world as another human being sees it; we cannot get inside the other's experience and know and feel it from such a viewpoint. For all the thought experiments one might construct about such a possibility, to really inhabit the other would involve a merging wherein the resulting whole would be a new being rather than the inhabitor experiencing the other's experiences. That being said, one may yearn for such merging, especially when one is in love.

In this regard, experiencing the other through art is the nearest we can come to such merging. For the artwork at least does more than describe the other's perspective on things; it shows the artist's vision sensuously and imaginatively in a way that allows us to identify with it, yet without being psychologically pressured to do so. Aesthetic empathy of this kind involves our dwelling alongside and with the other; and again, this points toward the divine. Of course, since we are finite, we cannot sufficiently inhabit the Godhead. What we feel of the divine nature comes through our wonder at the distinctiveness of human consciousness in terms of its place in nature—as the phenomenon that opens the temporal horizon described earlier. Through this we can empathize with aspects of divine being and discern our crude kinship with God the creator, thus participating symbolically in aspects of that Supreme Being's creative spirit. The experience of art points us in this very direction—if we have faith.

## Conclusion

We have seen that through the visibility of pictorial art, we might be said to exist as an image of God the creator in complex ways. *Contra* Marion, the religious meaning of painting only emerges insofar as it affirms rather than effaces its own visibility, and it can do this only through existing as art.

Again, it must be emphasized that this religious interpretation requires a leap of faith. But there is a further reason to take such a leap. Some take the phenomenon of religion itself to be based on consolatory beliefs derived from semimythic narratives wherein, in effect, the survival instinct tries to overcome the threat of death and extinction as such. But while the leap of faith just described finds inspiration in such narratives, it is not reducible to them. It centers, rather, on the contextualizing of independently established metaphysical truths concerning what it is to be self-conscious and to make pictorial art.

If we are puzzled as to why these truths hold—why the universe has come to exist in just this way—then we are entitled to countenance a more comprehensive dimension of truth that might explain their emergence. We want to know why it is that the universe has this specific metaphysical structure and significance. In such a context, the leap of faith is a rational thing, and pictorial art embodies metaphysical truths that point us toward it. Pictorial art's aesthetic transcendence completes us.

In this context it is worth making a few comments on the significance of the beautiful and the sublime as such. The phenomenon of beauty in its most basic sense involves a pleasure in the structure of appearance that centers on factors such as the relation between unity and diversity in the phenomenal manifold. Such beauty can be enjoyed for its own sake because of the stimulation it affords our cognitive faculties. There are more specific modes of it—such as pictorial beauty—where our pleasure in the relation between parts and whole is mediated through reference to the kind of thing that sustains the relation.[4] Through this, our cognitive inherence in the world and our relations with others can be felt as well as comprehended, which makes the feeling involved into more than just a pleasurable sensation. It can be sought out and cultivated, and is also an experience whose grounds in the particular case can be explained to others.

Reflection upon beautiful things and on our relation to them plays an important role in how they are experienced. Beauty illuminates the basic fit between our cognitive capacities and the phenomenal world in ways that refer as well to who and what we are and our relation to Being (a feature that is, of course, especially central to pictorial and other modes of artistic beauty). Through this enhanced complementarity of rational and sensible basics, we exist in a more complete way.

Beauty, then, is one of the ways in which the universe is rendered meaningful. And the character of this meaning centers on an adaptedness of cognition to the world, which in the context of faith can be regarded as a sign of divine purposiveness in nature. This sense of purposiveness is even more enhanced in the case of ideal and metaphysical beauty in visual art, where our pleasure centers on aesthetic transcendence. The particular work, in the quality of its particularity, refers us both to a logic of being bound up with the fundamental structure of space and to the symbolic transcendence of the limits of our finitude—a factor that allows us to exist (however crudely) in God's image.

The sublime, in all its modes, has a similar meaning. The scope of our rational being is made vivid through natural phenomena or representations of them that emphasize the physical limitations of our embodiment. In the context of faith, this is a sign of the divine within us, but it can also be the basis of a further—specifically religious—mode of the sublime. For while the human power to comprehend what physically exceeds us on such a vast scale is sublime, even more so is the fact that this excess is created and contained by the Supreme Being. What we only understand as an idea is something, as it were, metaphysically contained by God.

This leaves us, however, with a final and surprising conclusion. Because beauty and sublimity in all their modes are positive features of experience, some have imagined that God—as the source of all perfections and so on— must be beautiful and sublime in absolute terms. This does not follow; indeed, it reverses the religious significance of aesthetic experience. Inasmuch as God creates and sustains human reality, then how it is experienced is known to God. The Supreme Being knows what we feel and experience. However, the whole point of aesthetic experiences as viewed in the context of faith is that they are modes of discovering signs of God in the phenomenal world; they are a vehicle to transcendence. But God is already transcendent. The Supreme Being is not an embodiment of beauty and the sublime; considered theologically, these experiences are no more than idioms wherein finite creatures intuitively discern ways in which they are made in the image of God.

Put simply, the Supreme Being is beyond all notions of beauty and sublimity. Those modes of aesthetic experience are divine gifts to us. In the final analysis, and in the context of faith, aesthetic transcendence, beauty, and sublimity are routes to the understanding of who and what we are in relation to God. Through this, we find ultimate completeness.

# NOTES

## Introduction

1. Nelson Goodman, *Languages of Art*, 2nd ed. (New York: Hackett, 1976). Goodman's denial of resemblance's playing a necessary role in pictorial representation was found especially provocative.

2. Kendall Walton, *Mimesis as Make-Believe* (Cambridge, Mass.: Harvard University Press, 1990 (a wide-ranging book that goes beyond exclusively pictorial issues); Robert Hopkins, *Picture, Image and Experience: A Philosophical Inquiry* (Cambridge: Cambridge University Press, 1998); Dominic MacIver Lopes, *Understanding Pictures* (Oxford: Oxford University Press, 1996); Patrick Maynard, *drawing distinctions: the varieties of graphic expression* (Ithaca, N.Y.: Cornell University Press, 2005).

3. See Maurice Merleau-Ponty, *Philosophy and Painting: The Merleau-Ponty Aesthetics Reader*, ed. Galen Johnson (Evanston, Ill.: Northwestern University Press, 1993); Gilles Deleuze, *Francis Bacon: The Logic of Sensation*, 2nd ed. (London: Continuum, 2005); Jean-Luc Nancy, *The Ground of the Image*, trans. Jeff Fort (New York: Fordham University Press, 2005); and Jacques Rancière, *The Future of the Image*, trans. Geoffrey Elliott (London: Verso, 2007).

4. Ernst Gombrich, *Art and Illusion: A Study in the Psychology of Pictorial Representation* (London: Phaidon Press, 1960). For Elkins, see especially *On Pictures and the Words That Fail Them*, 2nd ed. (Cambridge: Cambridge University Press, 2011).

5. Richard Wollheim, *Painting as an Art* (London: Thames and Hudson, 1987); Dominic MacIver Lopes, *Sight and Sensibility: Evaluating Pictures* (Oxford: Clarendon Press, 2005).

6. See, for example, *Phenomenologies of Art and Vision: A Post-Analytic Turn* (London: Bloomsbury, 2013). In Chapters 1 and 2, I offer extended analyses and critique of Wollheim.

7. Wollheim describes what I am describing here as "seeing-in" and discusses it at length throughout *Painting as an Art*. Interestingly, much of the recent philosophical debate concerning pictorial representation centers, in effect, on the roles played by visual perception and cultural convention in seeing-in. See, for example, the range of essays in C. Abell and K. Bantinaki, eds., *Philosophical Perspectives on Depiction* (Oxford: Oxford University Press, 2010).

8. Lyotard's ideas on these topics can be found in the postscript to *The Postmodern*

*Condition: A Report on Knowledge*, trans. Geoff Bennington and Rachel Bowlby (Manchester, U.K.: Manchester University Press, 1984); and in chapters 6, 7, and 11 of *The Inhuman*, trans. Geoffrey Bennington and Rachel Bowlby (Cambridge: Polity Press, 1991). My detailed criticisms of Lyotard can be found in chapters 8 and 9 of *Critical Aesthetics and Postmodernism* (Oxford: Clarendon Press, 1993).

9. For Kant's theory of fine art (which is not, however, specifically visual), see his *Critique of the Power of Judgment*, trans. Paul Guyer and Eric Matthews (Cambridge: Cambridge University Press, 1999), bk. 1, secs. 43–53, pp. 182–207. Schopenhauer's more important comments on visual art can be found in *The World as Will and Representation*, trans E. J. Payne (New York: Dover, 1967), vol. 2, secs. 45–48, pp. 220–233. The Stanford Encyclopedia entry on "Schopenhauer's Aesthetics" by Sandra Shapshay is an excellent introduction to this material; see http://plato.stanford.edu/entries/schopenhauer-aesthetics/. Hegel's most detailed analyses of painting are in his *Aesthetics*, vol. 2, *Part III: The System of the Individual Arts*, trans. T. M. Knox (Oxford: Clarendon Press, 1975), pp. 797–887.

10. Mary Mothersill, *Beauty Restored* (Oxford: Oxford University Press, 1984); Nick Zangwill, *The Metaphysics of Beauty* (Ithaca, N.Y.: Cornell University Press, 2001).

11. Jennifer A. McMahon, *Aesthetics and Material Beauty* (London: Routledge, 2007); McMahon's method is that of a "critical aesthetic realism," which is articulated in the fullest terms in her "Conclusion: An Ontology of Art," pp. 177–199. Elaine Scarry, *On Beauty and Being Just* (Princeton, N.J.: Princeton University Press, 1999); Alexander Nehamas, *Only a Promise of Happiness: The Place of Beauty in a World of Art* (Princeton, N.J.: Princeton University Press, 2007); Arthur Pontynen, *For the Love of Beauty: Art History and the Moral Foundations of Aesthetic Judgment* (New Brunswick, N.J.: Transaction, 2006). Pontynen's treatment of aesthetic empathy (pp. 109–112) follows the historical origins of the notion of empathy rather too closely; in the present work, I will argue that aesthetic empathy should be understood in much broader terms, on the basis of artistic style.

12. Robert Clewis, *The Kantian Sublime and the Revelation of Freedom* (Cambridge: Cambridge University Press, 2009). As well as providing a wealth of tenacious analyses and arguments, this book serves scholarship on the Kantian sublime further still through its appendix 3, which lists all the examples of the sublime provided by Kant and the relevant category to which he assigns them.

13. Kirk Pillow, *Sublime Understanding: Aesthetic Reflection in Kant and Hegel* (Cambridge, Mass.: MIT Press, 2003). Pillow in effect uses Kant's theory in a very broad way—"I privilege sublime reflection in particular because it best models our interpretative search for meaning in things" (p. 4). My own approach, in contrast, emphasizes the sublime only in relation to aesthetic transcendence.

14. Emily Brady, *The Sublime in Modern Philosophy: Aesthetics, Ethics, and Nature* (Cambridge: Cambridge University Press, 2013). For my discussion of her in the present text, see the beginning of Chapter 4.

15. Simon Morley, ed., *The Sublime: Documents of Contemporary Art* (London: Whitechapel Art Gallery, 2010); Luke White and Claire Pajaczkowska, eds., *The Sublime*

*Now* (Cambridge: Cambridge Scholars, 2009); Roald Hoffmann and Iain Boyd Whyte, eds., *Beyond the Finite: The Sublime in Art and Science* (New York: Oxford University Press, 2011). The last-mentioned work here is exceptional in that, while it does not elucidate the distinctively pictorial articulation of the sublime (which, of course, is not its remit), it makes an outstanding contribution to issues bound up with aesthetic transcendence as such across a range of contexts.

16. Richard Harries, *Art and the Beauty of God: A Christian Understanding* (London: Mowbray, 1993); Richard Viladesau, *Theological Aesthetics: God in Imagination, Beauty, and Art* (Oxford: Oxford University Press, 1999). Viladesau's book is marvelous in terms of its intellectual sweep and a source of many fine insights. My position, however, holds that if we are to establish the theological significance of the arts, it will be through close analysis of the ontologies of the individual art media rather than through notions that encompass them all. One writer who takes some steps in this direction is Pavel Florensky, an Orthodox priest who devoted considerable attention to the metaphysical analysis of visual artworks as visual. His position is religiously conservative but adventurous in its application. See, for example, his *Beyond Vision: Essays on the Perception of Art* (London: Reaktion, 2002); the chapter on "Reverse Perspective" is especially provocative, not least because of its attempt to make a hierarchical distinction between linear and reverse perspective, to the benefit of the latter. Another generally useful volume is Daniel J. Treier, Mark Husbands, and Roger Lundin, eds., *The Beauty of God: Theology and the Arts* (Downers Grove, Ill.: IVP Academic, 2007).

17. T. J. Gorringe, *Earthly Visions: Theology and the Challenges of Art* (London: Yale University Press, 2011), p. 191.

18. Ibid., p. 192.

19. Jean-Luc Marion, *The Crossing of the Visible*, trans. James K. A. Smith (Stanford, Calif.: Stanford University Press, 2004), p. ix.

*Chapter 1*

1. Plato, *Republic*, trans. Robin Waterfield (Oxford: Oxford University Press, 1993), p. 353.

2. See *Republic* 597; ibid., pp. 346–348.

3. Ibid., pp. 224–225. Erwin Panofksy offers a useful discussion of this passage in his *Idea: A Concept in Art Theory* (New York: Harper and Row, 1968), pp. 3–4.

4. Plato, *Republic*, p. 225.

5. Plotinus, *The Enneads*, trans. Stephen MacKenna (New York: Larson, 1992), p. 485.

6. Ibid., p. 486.

7. Leon Alberti, *On Painting*, trans. Cecil Grayson (London: Penguin, 1991), p. 90.

8. Ibid., p. 91.

9. Arthur Schopenhauer, *The World as Will and Representation*, trans. E. F. J. Payne, vol. 1 (New York: Dover Publications, 1967), p. 222; italics in original.

10. Joshua Reynolds, *Discourses on Art* (London: Collier-Macmillan, 1969), p. 31. For a stimulating broader context for these remarks and the ideal in general, see the

chapter on "Classicism" in Karsten Harries' *Meaning of Modern Art: A Philosophical Interpretation* (Evanston, Ill.: Northwestern University Press, 1968).

11. Reynolds, *Discourses on Art*, p. 44.

12. Ibid., pp. 45–46.

13. Ibid., p. 46.

14. Ibid., p. 50.

15. Ibid., p. 58.

16. Ibid., p. 56.

17. Ibid., p. 50.

18. For Locke's theory, see his *An Essay Concerning Human Understanding*, vol. 2 (London: Everyman Library, 1974), pp. 15–26.

19. Reynolds, *Discourses on Art*, p. 47.

20. Ibid., p. 48.

21. Locke, *An Essay Concerning Human Understanding*, p. 17.

22. George Berkeley, *A New Theory of Vision and Other Writings* (London: Dent, 1969), p. 98.

23. In his interesting book *The Political Theory of Painting from Reynolds to Barry* (New Haven, Conn.: Yale University Press, 1987), John Barrell offers a sustained genealogical analysis of the relation between the ideas in Reynolds' *Discourses* and the sociopolitical and economic context that influences his doctrines. Barrell admirably avoids the reductionist tendency of many such approaches, but he does not engage much with the enduring significance of Reynolds' ideas.

24. I have tried in this chapter to be as sympathetic as possible to Reynolds' treatment of his central concepts. This should not hide the fact that, overall, there is much in Reynolds that is rather more problematic in logical terms than I have been able to show. For an investigation of some of these difficulties, see Gunter Leypoldt's "A Neoclassical Dilemma in Sir Joshua Reynolds's Reflections on Art," *British Journal of Aesthetics* 39, no. 4 (1999): pp. 330–349. Despite the seemingly narrow scope of its title, this article manages to explore a surprising number of interrelated difficulties in Reynolds' thought.

25. Heinrich Wolfflin, *Principles of Art History*, trans. M. Hottinger (New York: Dover Publications, 1950), p. 14.

26. Ibid., p. 15.

27. For a discussion of the aesthetic achievement of expressionist tendencies, see chapter 3 of my *The Phenomenology of Modern Art: Exploding Deleuze, Illuminating Style* (London: Continuum, 2012).

## Chapter 2

1. Interestingly, a picture's surface merely *looks* two-dimensional. Nothing in the physical world, however, is two-dimensional in any absolute sense; such dimensionality has only ideal or virtual existence. This means that the picture's physical surface has an ambiguous status, for while we must consider the way in which the marks or inscriptions "sit" upon the surface in order to recognize the kind of medium involved (painting, drawing, or whatever) or to determine the picture's style, the physical character of

the surface is, nevertheless, not essential to its status as a picture. All that is required for pictorial status is the aforementioned virtual planar structure and the recognizable three-dimensional content that it is taken to communicate.

2. Heinrich Wölfflin holds that different approaches to this strategy may be used to distinguish major stylistic tendencies. See his *The Principles of Art History*, trans. M. D. Hottinger (New York: Dover Publications, 1950), pp. 73–123.

3. To the best of my knowledge, the first to distinguish between the external and internal observer of a picture was Alois Riegl; the distinction operates throughout his key work *The Group Portraiture of Holland* (San Diego: Getty Research Institute, 2000). Wollheim makes use of a similar distinction throughout his *Painting as an Art*.

4. The points made here are true even of pictures based on photographs, such as the superrealist painting that was popular in the early 1970s. For one thing, these pictures differ in scale from both the photographs they are based on and the material captured in the photograph. Of course, one might create such a work that was perceptually indistinguishable from a photograph, but in such a case, we would perceive it mistakenly as a photograph and not as a picture.

5. The classic account is in book 11 of St. Augustine's *Confessions*, trans. Henry Chadwick (Oxford: Oxford World's Classics, 2008), pp. 221–245. A dedicated study of the topic is George Herbert Mead's unfinished *The Philosophy of the Present* (New York: Prometheus Books, 2002).

6. This is the view put forward in Erwin Panofsky's celebrated *Perspective as Symbolic Form*, trans. Christopher Wood (New York: Zone Publications, 1991). Panofsky presents these as empirical aspects of picturing's historical development. However, there is also a case for seeing them (individually or in combination) as the conceptual basis for organizing pictorial space.

7. The flattening of three-dimensional aspects by art organized on the basis of planar unity is very characteristic of Byzantine and medieval art. It marks a kind of favoring of spiritual values over the corporeal richness of the material world.

8. A wide-ranging discussion of this problem can be found in Robert Hopkins' *Painting, Image and Experience: A Philosophical Inquiry* (Cambridge: Cambridge University Press, 1998), pp. 152–158. An excellent account of the historical development and conceptual implications of linear perspective can be found in chapter 2 of Patrick Maynard's *drawing distinctions: the varieties of graphic method* (Ithaca, N.Y.: Cornell University Press, 2005).

9. See Maurice Merleau-Ponty, *The Merleau-Ponty Aesthetics Reader: Philosophy and Painting*, ed. Galen A. Johnson and Michael B. Smith (Evanston, Ill.: Northwestern University Press, 1993), p. 87, for a more negative interpretation of this systematicity.

10. Hubert Damisch has argued for some interesting links between grammar and perspective in his *The Origins of Perspective*, trans. John Goodman (Cambridge, Mass.: MIT Press, 1995).

11. Gareth Evans, *Varieties of Reference* (Oxford: Clarendon Press, 1982), p. 176.

12. Richard Wollheim, *Painting as an Art* (London: Thames and Hudson, 1987), p. 46.

13. In my book *The Transhistorical Image: Philosophizing Art and Its History* (Cam-

bridge: Cambridge University Press, 2002). See, for example, my discussions of Bell and Fry, chap. 1, pp. 8–11; and Greenberg, chap. 1, pp. 16–20.

14. Clive Bell, *Art* (London: Chatto and Windus, 1914), pp. 69–70.

## Chapter 3

1. The interpretation of Kant's theory of the sublime offered in the present chapter is a further development of ideas from chapter 7 of *The Kantian Aesthetic: From Knowledge to the Avant-Garde* (Oxford: Oxford University Press, 2010), pp. 173–198.

2. See sections 25–28 inclusive in book 1 of Immanuel Kant, *The Critique of the Power of Judgment*, trans. Paul Guyer and Eric Matthews (Cambridge: Cambridge University Press, 2000).

3. Emily Brady, *The Sublime in Modern Philosophy: Aesthetics, Ethics, and Nature* (Cambridge: Cambridge University Press, 2013), p. 120. Other skeptics concerning the sublime as an artistic concept include James Elkins, "Against the Sublime," in *Beyond the Infinite: The Sublime in Art and Science* (Oxford: Oxford University Press, 2011), pp. 75–90; and Jane Forsey, "Is a Theory of the Sublime Possible?," *Journal of Aesthetics and Art Criticism* 65, no. 4 (2007): pp. 381–389. Elkins emphasizes the importance of specific historical contexts and argues that the sublime cannot be effectively employed as a concept beyond these. My point, however, is that Kant's theory of the sublime (however awkwardly he presents it) is based on a cognitive structure that is basic to us as finite embodied beings. It consists in the fact that phenomenally or psychologically overwhelming phenomena can make the extraordinary scope of rational comprehension vivid to the senses. This can be instantiated differently under different historical conditions—there are, in other words, different modes of the sublime—but it is the same cognitive structure that is at issue in each of them. I offer further grounds for understanding the sublime as an artistic concept in chapter 7 of *The Kantian Sublime: From Morality to Art* (Clarendon Press, Oxford, 1989), pp. 153–174.

4. I think Kant's general strategy on this is very sound; see my discussion of his transcendental deduction and the schematism in chapters 1 and 2 of *The Kantian Aesthetic*, pp. 9–34 and 35–59, respectively.

5. Kant, *Critique*, p. 138.

6. I offer a detailed analysis of its twists and turns in chapter 4 of *The Kantian Sublime*, pp. 78–107.

7. Kant, *Critique*, p. 135.

8. Ibid., p. 141.

9. Blaise Pascal, *Pensees*, trans. J. Warrington (London: Dent, 1973), p. 110.

10. Kant, *Critique*, p. 145.

11. This where my approach comes closest to Kirk Pillow's. He points out that "Kant's theory of the sublime does in principle allow inclusion of any number of contextual or other nonformal considerations that may contribute to elaborating meanings for works"; see Pillow, *Sublime Understanding*, p. 66.

12. I explore the relation between deconstruction, complexity, and the sublime in part 2 of *Critical Aesthetics and Postmodernism* (Oxford: Clarendon Press, 1993).

13. "Cultural criticism finds itself faced with the final stage of the dialectic of culture and barbarism. To write poetry after Auschwitz is barbaric. And this corrodes even the knowledge of why it has become impossible to write poetry today. Absolute reification, which presupposed intellectual progress as one of its elements, is now preparing to absorb the mind entirely"; Theodor W. Adorno, *Prisms*, trans. Samuel Weber and Sherry Weber (Cambridge, Mass.: MIT Press, 1981), p. 34.

14. From "Gleaning in History, or Coming After/Behind the Reapers: The Feminine, the Stranger and the Matrix in the Work of Bracha Lichtenberg," in *Generations and Geographies in the Visual Arts: Feminist Readings*, ed. Griselda Pollock (London: Routledge, 2005), p. 363.

15. Ibid.

## Chapter 4

1. Mark Rothko, quoted in John Fischer, "The Easy Chair: Mark Rothko, Portrait of the Artist as an Angry Man" (1970), reprinted in *Mark Rothko: Writings on Art*, ed. M. Lopez-Ramiro (New Haven, Conn.: Yale University Press, 2005), p. 133.

2. See, for example, my chapter on "Meaning in Abstract Art: From *Ur*-Nature to the Transperceptual," in *Meanings of Abstract Art: Between Nature and Theory*, ed. Paul Crowther and Isabel Wunsche (London: Routledge, 2012), pp. 70–82. The theory is developed in a broader context in chapters 8 and 9 of my *The Phenomenology of Modern Art: Exploding Deleuze, Illuminating Style* (London: Continuum, 2012); and in chapter 6 of *Phenomenology of the Visual Arts (even the frame)* (Stanford, Calif.: Stanford University Press, 2009). I prefer the term "abstract" to "nonfigurative" or "nonobjective" because I take such work to be figurative in an allusive way and to be concerned with visual factors that allow objects and states of affairs to become visible; the term "abstract" is more neutral.

3. The account that follows is a slightly edited and adapted version of that presented in chapter 9 of Crowther, *The Phenomenology of Modern Art*, pp. 240–242.

4. Actually, while Clyfford Still has the "all-over," large-scale approach, his work is focused on colored shapes per se rather than—as with Newman and Rothko—broader areas of grounding color animated by lines and bands. Yves Klein painted a number of blue color-field works, but their saturated intensity and small-scale relief effects do not involve any visual animation of the field itself. The first art historian to follow up the link between color-field painting and the sublime was Robert Rosenblum; see his article "The Abstract Sublime," *Art News* 59 (February 1961): pp. 38–41. He also discusses the importance of the sublime in abstract art and other contexts in his fine book *Modern Painting and the Northern Romantic Tradition: From Friedrich to Rothko* (London: Thames and Hudson, 1978); and in "Rothko's Sublimities," in *On the Sublime: Mark Rothko, Yves Klein, James Turrell* (Berlin: Deutsches Guggenheim Museum, 2001), pp. 41–59. T. J. Gorringe considers the religious meaning of Rothko and Newman in his discussion of abstract art in *Earthly Visions: Theology and the Challenges of Art* (London: Yale University Press, 2011). Interestingly, he selects Rothko's *Light Red over Black* (1957), which I will discuss a bit further on. However, Gorringe does not offer a detailed

analysis of the pictures but deploys instead some telling comments about them made by important interpreters of Rothko and Newman, such as Diane Waldstein (p. 185). Emily Brady considers Newman and Rothko in the course of her discussion of "Sublime Metaphysics and Art" in *The Sublime in Modern Philosophy: Aesthetics, Ethics, and Nature* (Cambridge: Cambridge University Press, 2013), pp. 132–142. She says of them that "despite their reference to something beyond themselves, the boundaries of these works ultimately limit their force" (p. 139). However, as shown in the previous chapter, Brady's strategy is stipulative: whether the limits she describes are operative is contingent on the taste and sensitivity of the spectator rather than something intrinsic to the works themselves. Indeed, we will see shortly exactly how these limits are exceeded.

5. John P. O'Neill, ed., *Barnett Newman: Selected Writings and Interviews* (Berkeley: University of California Press, 1992), p. 280. The most useful introduction to the theoretical aspect of Newman's work is Eva Ehninger's "'Man is Present': Barnett Newman's Search for the Experience of the Self," in Crowther and Wunsche, *Meanings of Abstract Art*, pp. 141–157. Her chapter is especially useful in describing some of the other ways that the figure/ground relation in Newman has been understood.

6. O'Neill, *Barnett Newman*, pp. 276–277.

7. Ibid., p. 190.

8. This reading is supported by remarks in ibid., p. 190.

9. Yves-Alain Bois's influential catalogue essay "Perceiving Newman," in *Barnett Newman: Paintings; April 8–May 7, 1998* (New York: Pace Gallery, 1988), suggests that Newman's career follows "a sort of phenomenological inquiry into the nature of perception" (p. 5). Specifically, he holds that in Newman's work, the relation between the zip and ground is one of irreconcilability—"we cannot both fix the zip and look at the painting at the same time, and it is precisely upon this impossibility that Newman based the dazzling effects of his canvasses" (p. 7). One might argue, however, that it is precisely when we fix the zip as something painted that we see the painting as painting per se. Indeed, the oscillating relation between figure and ground (which will be shown to be central to Newman's work) is not a case of irreconcilability but complementarity. Figure and ground in perception change constantly: as our attention changes, what was figure may become ground and vice versa. What Newman really does through his zips is to explore this flexibility in ways that exemplify metaphysical significance. Bois does not negotiate this.

10. Maurice Merleau-Ponty, *Phenomenology of Perception*, trans. Colin Smith with revisions by Forrest Williams (London: Routledge and Kegan Paul, 1974), p. 170.

11. O'Neill, *Barnett Newman*, p. 190.

12. According to Fischer's account, Rothko claimed that his somber color scheme was chosen so as to "ruin the appetite of every son of a bitch who eats in that room"; see Rothko, *Writings on Art*, p. 131.

13. The paintings are beautifully reproduced as color plates 62–70 (inclusive) in the exhibition catalogue *Mark Rothko: 1903–1970* (London: Tate Gallery, 1987).

14. Rothko, *Writings on Art*, p. 131.

15. "Notes from a conversation with Selden Rodman, 1956," in ibid., pp. 119–120.

*Chapter 5*
1. For some further reflections upon the end-of-art problem, see the conclusion to my *Defining Art, Creating the Canon: Artistic Value in an Era of Doubt* (Oxford: Oxford University Press, 2012), pp. 235–246.
2. Jürgen Habermas, "Modernity—An Incomplete Project," in *Postmodern Culture*, ed. Hal Foster (London: Pluto Press, 1985), p. 13.
3. Ibid.
4. For useful discussions of the ontology of photography and its broader existential implications, see, respectively, Jonathan Friday's *Aesthetics and Photography* (London: Ashgate, 2002); and Roland Barthes's *Camera Lucida: Reflections on Photography*, trans. Richard Howard (London: Jonathan Cape, 1982).
5. An influential compendium of cybertheory is Neil Spiller's *Cyber Reader: Critical Writings for the Digital Era* (London: Phaidon, 2002).
6. Jos de Mul, "Virtual Reality: The Interplay Between Technology, Ontology, and Art," in "Proceedings of the XIVth International Congress of Aesthetics," pt. 1, special issue, *Filozofski Vestnik* 20, no. 2 (1999): pp. 175–176.

*Chapter 6*
1. Jean-Luc Marion, *The Crossing of the Visible*, trans. James K. A. Smith (Stanford, Calif.: Stanford University Press, 2004), p. ix.
2. Ibid.
3. Ibid., p. 4. In realizing this, Marion advances considerably beyond Merleau-Ponty's influential and highly critical understanding of perspective. As the basis of his critique, Merleau-Ponty invests a huge amount in the prereflective character of our spatial orientation. In it, no explicit distinction is made between the subject and object of experience; indeed, his later work emphasizes that subject and world share the same perceptual "flesh" and are aspects of one another. All well and good. But while, psychologically speaking, our ordinary negotiation of the spatial world does not involve occurrent knowledge of its ideality, it is logically presupposed that we have acquired such knowledge at some point. In order to act, think, and feel in a human way, one must be able, as circumstances demand, to articulate an explicit sense of one's own position and potential as one object among others in a space whose contents reconfigure in systematic correlation with one's changes of position. This need not be expressed in scientific terms; it is just a basic practical recognition that the spatial world and our actions within it are not arbitrary but have a systematically unified correlation. Merleau-Ponty's main critique of perspective can be found in section 3 of the essay "Eye and Mind," in *The Merleau-Ponty Aesthetics Reader: Painting and Philosophy*, ed. Galen A. Johnson and Michael B. Smith (Evanston, Ill.: Northwestern University Press, 1993), pp. 130–139.
4. Marion, *The Crossing of the Visible*, pp. 56–57. Merleau-Ponty also emphasizes the importance of the "invisible" in both painting and cognition. Marion's approach, however, is focused on the role of the gaze as an interpersonal factor in communication, whereas Merleau-Ponty emphasizes the "invisible" in relation to the usually unnoticed visual fabric of appearance. For Merleau-Ponty's account, see "Eye and Mind," pp. 127–128.

5. Marion, *The Crossing of the Visible*, p. 5.

6. Ibid., p. 9.

7. Ibid., pp. 9–10.

8. Ibid., pp. 11–12.

9. Ibid., pp. 36–37.

10. Ibid., p. 32.

11. Ibid., p. 36.

12. Ibid., p. 37.

13. Ibid., p. 25.

14. Ibid., p. 14.

15. Ibid., p. 16.

16. Ibid., p. 18.

17. Ibid., p. 19. Marion calls the work he is discussing here *White Square on a Black Base*, but there is no such work by Malevich. It becomes clear from his further discussion, however, that he's thinking of *White Square on a White Ground*.

18. Ibid., p. 19; emphasis in original.

19. Ibid., p. 34.

20. Ibid.

21. Ibid.

22. Ibid., p. 86. As this chapter progresses, it will become clear that Marion's understanding of the icon is very limited. For a much fuller account that does justice to all the features that Marion attempts to negotiate (and more besides), see Clemena Antonova's *Space, Time, and Presence in the Icon: Seeing the World with the Eyes of God* (Farnham, U.K.: Ashgate, 2007). The great strength of Antonova's book is its blending of conceptual factors with historical developments and broader cultural debates. It is particularly strong in its analysis of reverse perspective—a topic that Marion neglects (to his cost).

23. Marion, *The Crossing of the Visible*, p. 70.

24. Ibid., p. 20.

25. Ibid., p. 21.

26. Ibid., p. 59.

27. Ibid., p. 60.

28. Ibid., p. 61.

29. Ibid., p. 57.

30. Ibid.

31. Ibid., p. 58; emphasis in original.

32. Ibid., p. 3.

33. Ibid., p. 62. Oddly, Marion includes minimalism in this positive estimation, even though his earlier comments are negative. A similar inconsistency holds for his remarks concerning op art, which are positive at first and then reduced to "the stupid little virtualities of optic art" on page 41.

34. See ibid., p. 64.

35. Ibid., p. 27.

36. Ibid., p. 37.

37. Ibid., p. 63.

38. Ibid.

39. See, for example, Helmut Borsch-Supan's *Caspar David Friedrich* (London: Thames and Hudson, 1974).

40. He describes it, for example, as an "aesthetic asceticism"; see Marion, *The Crossing of the Visible*, p. 76.

41. Ibid., p. 65.

42. See Walter Benjamin, "The Author as Producer," included in a collection of Benjamin's essays titled *Understanding Brecht*, trans. Anna Bostock (London: Verso, 1998), pp. 185–204. I discuss this essay at length in chapter 4 of my *Critical Aesthetics and Postmodernism* (Oxford: Clarendon Press, 1993).

*Chapter 7*

1. I discuss the metaphysics of all this at great length in "The Limits of Objective Knowledge: What Mind-Independent Reality Must Be," chapter 6 of my book *Philosophy After Postmodernism: Civilized Values and the Scope of Knowledge* (London: Routledge, 2003).

2. A useful survey of some main points can be found in Jon Robson, "Aesthetic Testimony and the Norms of Belief Formation," *European Journal of Philosophy* (2013); doi:10.1111/ejop.12007.

3. "Pessimism" as a term in this context was originated by Robert Hopkins; see, for example, his article "How to Be a Pessimist About Aesthetic Testimony," *Journal of Philosophy* 108 (2011): pp. 138–157.

4. I explain this at much greater length in my discussions of Kant's pure aesthetic judgment in chapters 3 and 4 of *The Kantian Aesthetic: From Knowledge to the Avant-Garde* (Oxford: Oxford University Press, 2010).

# INDEX

abstraction (in art), 33, 78, 86, 105, 127
Adams, Ansell, 73
Adorno, Theodor W., 74, 167n13
aesthetic (as embodied in pictorial beauty) 2,
   4, 5, 6, 9; appreciation, 4, 115, 156; estimate,
   61; disinterestedness, 5; distinctiveness, 5,
   22, 32, 56, 149; feeling, 25, 59, 62, 69, 84, 93,
   102, 159; effects, 2; empathy, 5, 6, 157, 162n11;
   experience, 2, 4, 25, 53, 54, 55, 63, 70, 109,
   110; grounds, 2, 63; ideas, 7; judgment, 59,
   62, 156, 171n4; meaning, 36, 156; object, 5,
   111, 133, 156; symbolism, 86; testimony, 156,
   171nn2,3; transcendence, 2, 6, 7, 8, 25, 32, 37,
   52, 55, 57, 69, 96, 104–105, 115, 158, 159, 160,
   162n13, 163n15; significance, 2; unity, 4, 52,
   53, 158; uniqueness, 2, 4; see also, beauty
Alberti, Leon Battista, 13–14
allegorical, 19, 22
allusion, 83
allusive meaning (in abstract art), 79, 112, 123,
   167n2
Alexander the Great, 16
Alma-Tadema, Lawrence, 30
Andromache, 30–31
Antonova, Clemena, 170n22
Apollinian, 104
Apollo, 34
architecture, 3, 5
art: abstract, 33, 79–106, 112–113, 137, 167nn2,4;
   Byzantine, 45, 165; classic, 11, 26–36, 58;
   digital, 108, 109, 118–122, 124, 169n5; Gothic,
   139; historians, 31; history, 1, 20; medieval,
   45, 165; modern, 7, 44, 47, 48, 129–131, 133,
   135–136; optic, 170n33; pictorial, 1–10, 17, 19,
   22, 23, 37–56, 70, 71, 73, 78, 143–160
artistic, 2–4; analogy between artistic and
   divine creativity, 23, 151–158; composition,
   4, 14, 28, 33, 71, 115–116, 136, 152; creativity,

12, 15, 39–42, 71, 73, 74, 77, 114–116, 121–122,
   128–129, 141, 147, 148–150; expression, 2, 36,
   53–55, 87; meaning, 2, 4, 25, 28, 36, 108, 113,
   141, 142, 78–83, 85, 87–106, 152–158; medium,
   2, 3, 4, 5, 14, 16, 40, 41, 46, 51, 52, 53, 54, 55,
   71, 73, 74, 87, 107–124, 137, 146, 149, 152, 155,
   163n16, 164n1; status, 2, 116; style, 2, 4–6,
   14, 22, 24, 54–55, 71, 105, 120, 137–138, 145,
   148–149; technique, 73, 76, 118, 124; unity, 2,
   4–5, 6, 53, 147, 152–153, 154, 156
artwork, 16, 17, 34, 51, 52, 57, 58, 67, 69, 80, 83,
   85, 108, 151–157, 163n16; completed/finished,
   114, 140, 141, 148, 149, 152, 153, 155
associational meaning, 74, 82, 94, 102, 112
Auschwitz, 74, 77, 167n13

background plane. See plane, background
baroque, 139, 140
Barrell, John, 164n23
Barthes, Roland, 74, 169n4
beautiful, 2–3, 5, 6, 7, 8, 12–15, 18, 25, 158–160
beauty, 2–3, formal, 4, 54, 115; holistic, 6, 107,
   114–124, 152–153; ideal, 6, 11–36, 58; metaphys-
   ical, 37–56, 125, 159; pictorial, 1–10, 39, 111, 158
Being, 109, 114, 123, 124, 159
Bell, Clive, 54, 166n14
Benjamin, Walter, 142, 171n42
Berkeley, George, 18–19
Bernini, Gian Lorenzo; Ecstasy of St. Theresa, 73
body (human), 13, 18, 28, 29, 48, 65, 68, 69, 81,
   99, 122, 123, 124, 126, 135
Bois, Yves Alain, 168n9
Borsch-Supan, Helmut, 171n39
Bourgereau, William, 30
Brady, Emily, 8, 57–58, 70
brushstroke, 114, 136, 137, 149, 152
Burne-Jones, Edward Coley, Study for Love
   Among the Ruins, 22

caricature, 20
Carracci, Ludovico, 14
Caravaggio (Michelangelo Merisi da Caravaggio), 128, 139
cartoons, 20
causal, 39, 50, 73, 74, 110, 113, 114, 115, 116, 118, 120, 145
causal rigidity (in photography), 39–40, 73, 74, 110
Charles V, 11
chiaroscuro, 139
Chirico, Giorgio de, 32
Classic. *See* classic art
classical, 11, 15, 17, 31, 32, 34
Clewis, Robert, 8, 162n12
Coates, Peter, 35
cognition, 32, 41, 56, 78, 96, 159, 169n3
color, 4, 14, 17, 18, 21, 24, 28, 29, 30, 33, 35, 46, 47, 54, 82, 86–88, 93, 97, 102, 103, 105, 120, 121, 129, 167n4, 168n12
Colossus of Rhodes, 73
completion (aesthetic/metaphysical/psychological), 2, 5, 6, 25, 95, 104, 114–115, 123, 146, 148, 150–158. *See also* artwork, symbolic
composition: *See* artistic
computer, 99, 118, 119, 124. *See also* digital
concrete universal, 24–26, 33, 34, 36
conceptual, 8, 41, 48, 107, 128, 129, 165n8, 170n22
contextualism (in art history), 20
contingency, 113, 114, 148, 149, 152, 168
craftsman, 11, 12
creation. *See* artistic, *and* divine
creative, 23, 34, 74, 76, 77, 107, 119, 121, 122, 124, 129, 148, 149, 154, 157, 158
creativity. *See* artistic
critical judgment, 110, 137–138
crucifixion (of Christ), 67, 68, 87–96, 132–133
culture, 1, 7, 11, 16, 17, 21, 33, 41, 82, 116, 167n13, 169n2

Dalí, Salvador, 32
Damisch, Hubert, 165n10
Darkly, Arlo P., *The Terminator*, 112
David, Jacques-Louis, 26
death, 28, 67, 74, 153–154, 158
deconstruction, 74, 76, 116, 166n12
Delacroix, Eugène, 20
Delaroche, Paul, 30
Deleuze, Gilles, 1
digital imagery, 120–124
Dionysian, 104

divine, 49–52, 55, 56, 84, 85, 96, 105, 132, 150–155, 157–160; presence, 6, 8, 84, 95, 157; sensuous, 9, 19, 49, 51, 56. *See also* God, Godhead, religious, and Supreme Being
Duchamp, Marcel, 136

Ehninger, Eva, 168n5
El Greco, 128
Elkins, James, 1, 161n4, 166n3
embodiment (human), 23, 94, 95, 108, 121, 123, 159, 166n3
erotic, 31
Escher, M.C., 146
eternalization, 9, 50, 104, 105, 109, 114
Ettinger, Bracha Lichtenberg, 74–77, 108; *Autistwork n. 1*, 75; *Eurydice n. 23*, 75
Evans, Gareth, 48
existence, 4, 5, 25, 38, 39, 40, 62, 79, 83, 88, 93, 94, 134, 143–146, 151–153, 154, 155, 164n1
existential, 4, 23, 41, 53, 56, 74, 84, 85, 94, 95, 103, 105, 110, 119, 127, 132, 135, 155, 157, 169n4
experience, 40, 77, 109, 117, 121; (holistic structure of), 114–115, 123
experience-object, 111–124
experiential; flow, 114–115; matrix, 117–123; present, 41–42; structure, 115, 123
expression (see artistic expression)
expressive (qualities), 2, 53
faith (religious), 23, 52, 66, 68, 85, 96, 143, 150, 151, 158, 159, 160

female, 31, 43
feminist, 31, 167n14
figurative (pictorial content), 33, 79, 81, 97, 111, 115, 129, 131, 140, 167n2
figure/ground, 96, 168n5
finite limitations (of being human), 2, 4, 6, 25, 37, 49–52, 55, 56, 62, 84, 85, 95, 96, 104, 105, 108, 114, 132, 147, 150, 152–154, 158, 160, 166n3
finitude, 6, 49, 52, 56, 70, 78, 86, 105, 119, 159
Finlay, Ian Hamilton, 33–36; *Five Finials*, 35
Fischer, John, 167n1
Flaxman, John, 26
Florensky, Pavel, 163n16
foreground plane. *See* plane, foreground
foreshortening, 38
form; human, 28, 71; Platonic, 11–14, 23; significant, 54–55
formalism, 54
formal qualities, 115
Friday, Jonathan, 169n4

Friedrich, Caspar David, 139
Fry, Roger; *View of Royat from the Parc
  Montjuizot*, 47, 48, 54
future, 39–42, 45, 49, 50, 59, 113, 114, 118, 144–
  148, 151, 155,

Gauguin, Paul, 20, 23
gaze (the), 31, 43, 47, 48; in Marion, 126–128,
  130–134, 135, 136, 138, 139, 140, 141, 142, 169n4
gender, 135
genealogical, 20, 164n23
geometric immanence, 22–25, 26, 31, 32–34
Gérôme, Jean-Léon, 26, 30
gesture, 17, 29, 30, 34, 140, 148, 149, 152
Giotto, di Bondone, 11
God, 55–56, 84, 87, 95, 96, 105, 134, 138, 143,
  150, 150–158; is not beautiful or sublime,
  158–160
Godhead, 49, 52, 143, 158
Godhood, 52
Gombrich, Ernst, 1
Goodman, Nelson, 1
Gorringe, T.J., 8–9, 167–168n4
grand style; in Reynolds, 14–19, 20, 21
Greenberg, Clement, 54

Habermas, Jürgen, 109–110, 116
Hantai, Simon; *Tabula Rasa*, 130
Harries, Karsten, 164n10
Harries, Richard, 8
Hector (of Troy), 31
Hegel, Georg Wilhelm Friedrich, 7
Hegelian, 24
history painting, 17
Hoffman, Roald, 8, 163n15
holistic (structure of experience), 113–114
Holocaust (the)
Hopkins, Robert, 1, 165n8, 171n3
horizon: spatial, 38, 46, 73, 76, 99, 100; tempo-
  ral, 10, 42, 45, 51, 113, 114, 119, 143–146, 147,
  151, 158
human vocation, 64–65
Hunt, Alfred William, 71; *A Stream in a Moor-
  land Landscape*, 72, 73
Husserl, Edmund, 128

icon, 131–134, 138–141, 170n22
iconic, 118, 120; projection, 145–148
iconographical, 39, 69, 102, 113, 116
ideal. *See* beauty, ideal
Ideal (in Reynolds), 14–20

idealized, 22, 25, 32, 40, 41, 42, 46, 51, 52, 55, 86,
  93, 147
identity, 22, 84, 95, 103, 105, 114, 147, 148, 152
illusion, 56, 122–123, 127, 128, 129, 148; optical,
  80, 81, 83
image, 1, 8, 13–15, 19, 34, 39, 42, 43, 51, 58, 59,
  60–61, 74, 76, 77, 108, 110, 111, 115, 117, 145,
  148; digital, 117–124; existing in God's image
  through pictures, 50, 51–52, 56, 105, 150–158;
  in Marion, 125–141
imagination, 140, 141, 144, 145, 147, 149, 155, 156,
  157, 159
immanence. *See* geometric immanence
immanent, 151
immobilization (of time in pictures), 39, 40–
  42, 46, 49, 127. *See also* presentness
infinity, 25, 46, 51, 55, 56, 59, 128, 139, 142, 157; in
  Kant's theory of the sublime, 61–64
Ingres, Jean-Auguste-Dominique, 26, 30
intention, 3, 37; in Marion, 128–131, 137, 138, 146
intuitive, 13, 25, 46, 69, 83, 129, 136, 137, 160
invisible, 169n4; in Marion, 126–144

Jesus Christ, 26–28, *see also* crucifixion
John the Baptist, 28

Kant, Immanuel, 8, 57–70, 85, 162nn9,12,
  166nn1–11
Klein, Yves, 167n4
Kundera, Milan, 104

landscape, 4, 17, 20, 22, 44, 47–48, 71, 72, 73,
  139, 146
language, 85, 108, 109, 155–156
Leighton, Frederic Lord, 29–31; *Captive Andro-
  mache*, 30
Lessing, Gottfried, 16
Leypoldt, Gunther, 164n24
line, 4, 26, 54, 80, 95, 128, 129
literature, 3, 5, 53, 71, 149, 154, 155
Locke, John, 17–18
Lopes, Dominic McIver, 1
Lyotard, Jean-François, 7, 162n8

McMahon, Jennifer A., 7, 162n11
macroscopic, 144
Magritte, René, 32
making visible, 5–6, 102, 103, 104
Malevich, Kasimir, 32–33; *Self-Portrait*, 33, *Girl
  with a Red Pole*, 33; *White Square*, 134
Mantegna, Andrea, 26

maps, 51
Marion, Jean-Luc, 9, 125–142
Martin, John; *The Evening of the Deluge*, 71, 72, 73
Masaccio, 107
materials, 12, 19, 26, 33, 40, 41, 73, 79, 86, 108, 110, 112, 115, 116, 118, 120, 147, 149, 153, 154; in Reynolds, 14–18, 21
Maynard, Patrick, 1, 161n2, 165n8
Mead, George Herbert, 165n5
medium. *See* artistic, medium
memory, 15, 41, 76, 84, 121, 122, 141, 144–145, 149; bank, 119–120
Merleau-Ponty, Maurice, 1, 165n9, 168n10, 169n3
metaphorical, 19, 110, 115, 127
metaphysical, 6, 8, 13, 15, 23, 24, 33, 52, 54, 56, 58, 65, 83–85, 87, 94, 95–96, 102–105, 123, 126, 139, 143–160; 163n16, 168n9;(vis-à-vis the temporality of presentness), 39–42
Michelangelo (Buonarotti), 26, 31
microscopic, 144
modal plasticity, 147, 154
model, 30, 133, 137, 138, 150, 153, 162n13
modeled, 29, 33
modern, 47, 129, 135, 136
modernism, 136
modernist, 7, 44, 48, 133, 136
modernity, 109
moment, 16, 40, 41, 42, 49, 55, 71, 74, 76, 84, 93, 104–105, 109, 111, 113–115, 131, 148, 149
momentary, 39, 71, 103, 104, 105, 109, 111
Monet, Claude; *Rouen Cathedral*, 130, 131
monistic, 84, 95, 96, 103, 105
monism, 84
moral, 28, 34
Morley, Simon, 8
mortality, 74, 110
Mothersill, Mary, 7
movement, 29, 41, 42, 43–46, 48, 59, 126, 127
music, 3, 5, 53, 71, 152, 154, 155

Nain, Louis Le, 139
Nancy, Jean-Luc, 1
narrative, 4, 16, 18, 20, 22, 26, 28, 31, 45, 53, 55, 67, 69, 77, 87, 88, 111, 112, 115, 118, 121, 122, 123, 145, 153, 158
natural, 12, 14, 15, 16, 20, 24, 57, 58, 63, 64, 65, 67, 68, 69, 73, 82, 113, 127, 149, 159
naturalist, 20, 24, 32
nature, 8, 11, 12–15, 57, 58, 63–65, 71, 85, 149, 152, 157, 158, 159

Nazism, 34, 77
necessary, 95, 113, 114, 152
necessity, 61, 129, 148, 149, 152
Nehamas, Alexander, 7
Newman, Barnett, 86–96, 102–106; *Onement 1*, 86–87; *Stations of the Cross: First Station*, 89; *Stations of the Cross: Third Station*, 90, 167n4; *Stations of the Cross: Ninth Station*, 91; *Stations of the Cross: Tenth Station*, 92
Nietzsche, Friedrich, 104, 135
nude, 31

objectivity, 41, 48, 130, 133, 171n1
observer, 38, 46, 80, 104, 144–145
omniscience, 49–52, 55, 56, 157
ontological, 1–4, 17, 22, 24, 32, 40, 45, 54, 56, 73, 108, 111, 117, 121, 122, 123, 131, 136, 139, and metaphysics, 143–160
optical illusion, 80–83
original, 15, 132, 141, 149
originality, 20, 107, 129, 132, 136–138, 142, 149
orthogonals, 134
outline (in drawing and painting), 128

painting, 7, 8, 11, 12–36, 40, 47, 48, 70, 71, 76, 77, 79, 80, 86–106, 108, 109, 111, 113, 114–116, 117, 122, 123, 125–142, 148–150, 158, 164n1, 165n4, 167n4, 168nn9,13, 169n4
Pajaczkowska, Claire, 8
Panofsky, Erwin, 165n6
particularity, 141, 148, 149, 152, 156, 157, 159
parts. *See* whole/parts relation
perception, 3, 4, 6, 9, 15, 17–18, 22, 24–25, 26, 37, 38, 39–40, 43, 45, 46, 48, 50–52, 53, 65, 69, 70–71, 73, 77, 81, 93, 99, 103, 104, 106, 116, 123, 125, 126, 132, 134, 135, 140, 144, 148, 149, 153, 156, 161n7, 168n9; and the Kantian mathematical sublime, 58–64; and the transperceptual, 81–83
perspective in pictures, 37, 45–48, 55–56, 81, 108, 163n16, 165n8; in Marion's theory, 126–134, 135, 136, 138, 141, 142; in relation to divine consciousness, 51–52
phenomenality, (spatial and/or temporal ), 3, 4–5, 16, 22, 24, 31, 41–45, 59–61, 62, 65, 70, 71, 81, 84, 85, 105, 125, 139, 158, 159, 160
phenomenological, 9, 94, 115, 125, 168n9
photocollage, 110–111, 116, 117
photography, 3, 39–40, 73, 74–77, 109–116, 117, 118–124, 140, 169n4
Picasso, Pablo, 107

pictorial: content, 3, 16, 38, 41, 50, 147, 153; representation, 1–2, 3, 37–38, 78, 146, 154, 161n7; space, 26, 38, 43–48, 49–51, 55, 56, 83, 128, 134, 135, 146–147, 165n6. *See also* art, pictorial, and beauty, pictorial
Piero della Francesca, 45; *Baptism of Christ*, 26–28
piety, 33, 34; vulgar, 142
Pillow, Kirk, 8, 162n13, 166n11
planarity, 3, 4, 5, 26, 28, 30, 37–38, 42, 43, 45, 46, 52, 55, 56, 80, 83, 111, 126, 128, 135, 146, 153, 154, 165n7
plane: foreground/frontal, 30, 38, 43, 45, 47, 73, 100, 146, 147, 153; background, 38, 43, 73, 86, 119, 120, 129, 146, 148
planimetric, 26
plastic, 129
Plato, 9, 11–12, 14
Platonic, 23
Plotinus, 12–13
political, 20, 32, 33–34, 67, 77, 142, 164n23
Pollock, Griselda, 76, 167n14
Pollock, Jackson; *Full Fathom Five*, 82, 130
Pontynen, Arthur, 7, 162n11
possibility, 5, 6, 9, 10, 39–45, 49, 59, 126, 143–147
postmodern, 7, 9, 74, 161–162n8
Poussin, Nicholas, 26; *A Bacchanalian Revel Before a Term*, 28–29
Poynter, Sir Edward John, 26, 30
presence, 22, 25, 41, 104, 122, 136
present, the; 40–42, 45, 46, 48, 49–51, 56, 104, 113–115, 119, 144–148, 151
presentness, 40–42, 43, 45, 46, 48, 49–50, 52, 54, 55, 71, 94, 104, 109, 147
presumption of virtuality, 80, 93
printout, 118

question, the ultimate metaphysical, 83–85, 87, 88, 94, 95–96, 102–103, 105, 110,

Rancière, Jacques, 1
rationality, 15, 23, 83, 85–86, 94, 151, 152, 157, 158, 159; in Kant's theory of the sublime, 58–70, 166n3
reality, 8, 12, 28, 33, 39, 54, 73, 79, 80, 83–84, 86, 105, 128, 132, 147, 154, 171n1; virtual, 40, 118–123; ultimate, 54, 83–85, 86, 88, 93, 94–96, 102–106, 151, 160
reason, 12, 70, 77, 78, 84, 85, in Kant, 58–64, 66, 69, 70
recession in pictures, 26, 38, 43, 45, 50, 147, 153;

*see also* perspective in pictures, and pictorial space
reciprocal, 24–25, 41, 48, 113, 114, 123, 149
reciprocity, 24, 25, 28, 31, 51, 62, 104, 105–106, 123, 136, 141, 149, 150
reductionist, 164n23
re-encounterability (and self-consciousness), 48, 108
relativism, 7, 116
religion, 136, 158
religious factors, 7, 8–9, 10, 23, 33, 45, 51, 52, 54, 55, 56, 62, 66, 69, 70, 102; in relation to art, 125–160
Rembrandt (van Rijn), 19, 139
Renaissance, 25, 32, 45, 47
Representation. *See* pictorial, representation
resemblance, as a feature of pictures, 3, 37, 53
Reynolds, Sir Joshua, 14–24
Riegl, Alois, 165n3
Robson, Jon, 171n2
Rosenblum, Robert, 167n4
Rothko, Mark, 79, 86, 96–106; *Light Red over Black*, 98; *Black on Maroon*, 101; *Red on Maroon*, 101, 167n1, 167–168n4, 168n12
Rubens, Peter Paul, 19, 20, 139

St. Augustine, 165n5
St. Paul, 16
Scarry, Elaine, 7
schematic, 19–20, 119–120
Schopenhauer, Arthur, 7, 13–14, 162n9
sculpture, 3, 5, 12–13, 24, 73, 108, 139, 148
secular, 8, 10, 52, 55, 56, 125, 131
seeing-in (Wollheim), 3, 53, 161n7
self-consciousness, structure of, 5, 10, 48–49, 114, 120, 144, 149, 150
semantic, 1, 107
sensation, 159
sensory, 11, 57, 59, 60, 83, 120, 129–130, 133, 138, 145
sensuous divine. *See* divine, sensuous
shape, 3, 4, 18, 26, 35, 46, 47, 82, 93, 97, 102, 120, 121, 138, 144
Shapshay, Sandra, 162n9
sketch, 43, 128
space: occupancy, 4–5, 6, 23, 48, 50, 51, 52, 74, 83, 84, 86, 87, 94, 95, 96, 99, 100, 103–105, 106, 144–145, 146, 149, 150, 151, 153, 155, 169n3; physical, 46, 48, 94, 128, 135, 145, 148, 149, 150, 169n3; transperceptual (in abstract art), 81–83, 86, 93, 94, 99, 100–101, 102, 112,

167n2; virtual, 39, 123, 135, 148. *See also* pictorial space
spatial object, 3, 15, 22–24, 25, 26, 33, 39, 40, 42, 43, 45, 48, 49, 53, 81, 82, 103, 104, 111, 126, 128, 133, 139, 145, 147–148, 152, 153, 155; unity of, 3–4, 5, 53, 111–112, 147, 153
spectator of picture. *See* viewer
Spiller, Neil, 169n5
states-of-mind, 82, 88, 93, 94
Still, Clyfford, 86, 167n4
style, existential, 41; see also artistic
subject, embodied, 94, 108, 121, 123; and object of experience, 48–49, 169n3
subjective, 67, 123, 127, 138
subjectivity, 96, 117, transcendent 57–78
sublime, 6, 7, 8, 9, 57–58; dynamical, 59, 64–70, 77, 85, iconographic, 67–69, 74–78; mathematical, 59–64, 65, 66, 69, 70, 71, 85; pictorial, 57–78; mystical, 79–106, perceptual cues for, 58, 60–61, 63, 65, 69, 71
Supreme Being, 150–151, 159–160. *See also* divine, God, Godhead
surface of the drawing or painting, 3–4, 17, 43, 53, 71, 73, 80, 95, 103, 112, 114, 128, 129, 131, 141, 154, 164–165n1
symbolic, 2, 41, 50, 52, 74, 76, 77, 95, 96, 102, 116, 123, 147, 152, 153, 157; overcoming of finitude, 2, 6, 37, 41, 52, 54–55, 69, 105, 119, 152, 158, 159. *See also* completed/finished artwork, and completion (aesthetic/metaphysical/ psychological)
symbolic form, 117, 124
syntactic, 107
system (in the visible world), 46, 50, 51, 134
systematicity, (in relation to vision and perspective) 46–52, 135

temporal, 3, 10, 16, 39–42, 45, 51, 111, 115, 116, 117, 118, 120, 141, 148, 153–158; horizon, 143–146, 147–151, 152, 158
texture, 24, 33, 80, 121, 136
theistic, 9, 84, 95, 96, 103
theology of pictorial art, 125–160
Tintoretto (Jacopo Comin), *The Crucifixion*, 67
Tissot, James; *What Our Lord Saw from the Cross (Ce que voyait Notre-Seigneur sur la Croix)*, 68

Titian (Tiziano Vecellio), 11
token, 108
transcendence. *See* aesthetic, transcendence
transcendent, 17, 25, 62, 160, 166n4; subjectivity, 57–78
transhistorical, 16, 52, 165n13
Turner, Joseph Mallord William; *The Pass of St. Gothard*, 127
twofoldness, 53
type, 132, 155

ultimate. *See* question, the ultimate metaphysical, and reality, ultimate
uncanny, 34, 67, 85, 103, 110
uniqueness. *See* aesthetic, uniqueness, and artistic, uniqueness
universal, 24–25, 54. *See also* concrete universal
universality, 28, 96, 104, 105, 106
universe (the), 55, 63, 64, 83–84, 105; and the role of self-consciousness, 144–159

Van Gogh, Vincent, 23
vanishing point, 33, 45, 46, 134
viewer of the picture, 31, 34, 38, 42, 44, 45, 48, 49–50, 56, 67, 73, 76, 81, 82, 94, 102, 108, 125, 133, 135, 141, 146; external, 38, 42, 50; internal, 38, 39–41, 45–48, 49, 50–52
Viladesau, Richard, 8, 163n16
virtual reality (V-R), 40, 118, 122–123
visible. *See* making visible
visibility, 9, 125, 126–131, 133, 138, 140, 141, 158
vision, 50, 51, 52, 80–81, 127
volume; spatial, 33, 80, 82, 93, 144

Walton, Kendall, 1
Watts, George Frederick, 30
Weiss, Peter, 109
White, Luke, 8
whole/parts relation, 2–4, 21, 28, 49, 55, 60, 62, 70, 81, 93, 95, 103, 105, 111, 113–114, 129, 137, 148, 152, 157, 158
Whyte, Iain Boyd, 8, 163n15
Wolfflin, Heinrich, 26, 165n2
Wollheim, Richard, 2, 3, 53–54, 165n3

Zangwill, Nick, 7
Zurbaran, Francisco de, 19